TO

_____

FROM

_____

GOSPEL NOTES

-FOR-

ATHLETES, CLERGY, HEATHEN,
NERDS, POLITICIANS, REDNECKS,
&
SCIENTISTS

VOLUME I

FRED J. STONE

GOSPELNOTES: For - Atheists, Clergy, Heathen,
Nerds, Politicians, Rednecks & Scientists
Copyright @ 2020 by Fred J. Stone

All rights reserved. No part of this book may be reproduced, distributed, or transmitted in any form or by any means, including photocopying, recording, or other electronic or mechanical methods, except when individual notes are copied as free tracts.

* Some names and identifying details have been changed to protect the privacy of individuals.

* Although the author and publisher have made every effort to ensure that the information in this book was correct at press time, the author and publisher do not assume and hereby disclaim any liability to any party for any loss, damage, or disruption caused by errors or omissions.

* Scripture references are from the Revised Standard Version of 1952 unless otherwise indicated.

Cover design by Amber Stone

Printed in United States of America
IngramSpark Publishing
Publication Date: 2020-02-13
ISBN-13: 978-0-578-64645-9

CONTENTS

Introduction		7
1	Spiritual Stories	8
2	Words to Me 40 Yrs Ago	10
3	Wrestling With God	12
4	House Plants	14
5	Crowded Cities	16
6	Is That A Crutch?	18
7	I Saw The King	20
8	Elusive Things	22
9	Serving God	24
10	What About the Fruit?	26
11	Some Good Dope	28
12	Seven Wonders Of Heaven	30
13	The Gopher	32
14	Three Kinds Of Men *	34
15	The Endorsement	36
16	Seven Mysteries Of Life	38
17	Concerning Quicksand	40
18	The Date	42
19	Sad Facts Of Life	44
20	Set Yourself – Up	46
21	Soul Brothers	48
22	The Take Off	50
23	To Be A Man	52
24	Who Can You Trust?	54
25	Two Betrayals	56
26	The Underdog	58
27	The World	60
28	What's In It For Me?	62
29	Nation Of Cannibals *	64
30	Christian Giving	66
31	Roots	68
32	Religion Divides	70
33	My Miracles	72
34	Diabolic Churches	74
35	Freedom In Forgiveness	76
36	What Is Hypocrisy?	78
37	What Is Prayer?	80
38	What Is Marriage?	82
39	What Is Saved?	84
40	What Is Holiness?	86
41	What Is The Answer?	88
42	What Is Freedom?	90
43	The Demon	92
44	Invisible God	94
45	Four Kinds Of Pride	96
46	The Names Of Christ	98
47	The Holy Spirit	100
48	A Class Act	102
49	Which Church Is Right?	104
50	The Eagle	106
51	Being Your Own Boss	108
52	The Game *	110
53	Saying No To God	112
54	Invisible Wickedness	114
55	About Paying Taxes	116
56	New Age	118
57	Impostors	120
58	Famous Last Words	122
59	Patterns	124
60	Tragedy or Comedy?	126
61	Obsessions	128
62	Waxing Political	130
63	Old Age	132
64	What About Vengeance?	134
65	Why The Bible?	136
66	The Blessing & The Curse	138
67	Waxing Philosophical	140
68	Reasoning With God	142
69	The Praying Woman	144
70	The Chaplains	146
71	Ugly or Pretty?	148
72	God's Economics	150
73	Divine Presence	152
74	Why Literal?	154
75	Faith	156
76	"If I Were the Devil"	158
77	The Shakedown Oct '13	160
78	Frustrations	162
79	Rude Surprises	164
80	Illusions	166
81	The Commuter Flight	168
82	Church Vitality	170
83	Formula For Success	172
84	Unholy Cats	174
85	Looking Forward	176
86	Death Bed Confessions	178
87	Five C's of Romance *	180
88	Dog Eat Dog	182
89	Concerning Resale	184
90	Gifts & Rifts	186
91	The Brotherhood	188
92	Balance of Nature	190
93	In Defense of P. D.	192
94	Two Pictures	194
95	Realistic Expectations	196
96	What's In The Blood?	198
97	Was Jesus God?	200
98	Gravity	202
99	Too Many Questions	204
100	Common Conundrums	206

ACKNOWLEDGEMENTS

It is humbling to me to realize how many hours of computer time and talent that went into this manuscript. Those hours were done by my devoted wife (because I am a cave-man and don't touch the computer). Frances has spent literally years learning to use the computer. Then the cover design & polishing touch was from my daughter-in-law Amber to whom we are truly grateful. A certain amount of direction & encouragement came from an author friend Dr. Donald M. Minter, Flagstaff AZ. Last but not least for sure thanks go to the Holy Spirit who certainly hounded my mind with urgency to write most of these titles.

INTRODUCTION

It is my desire to have a perspective that avoids the narrow boundaries invented by teams of like minded theologians. - ("Religion Divides" - Note 32) "Cutting through the chase" is my goal and writing style. If these essays stir up interest in the Bible or Christ, and lead to even one(1) soul finding God, then I will be satisfied. These "Gospel-notes" can be used as free tracts. Just print them out on standard 8 1/2 x 11 printer paper, then fold them two times each way so that the title is on top. The index is link 0 which also prints out on standard paper. Feedback can be put on the Facebook page "Fred J Stone".

I was born & raised in South Phoenix, AZ. After graduating high school in '69, I joined the Army to be a helicopter mechanic/door gunner. I served a year in Viet Nam & made a deeper commitment to follow Christ in '72. God confirmed the relationship with many miracles. Then in '77 came a dynamic revelation of Jesus Christ in a spiritual dream ("I Saw the King" - Note 7). And I try to put my miracles & spiritual events into the fabric of the "notes". If those "events" are real, it would be wrong to forget or deny them. Interesting enough, those who call me a liar are usually established religious folk & ministers. (To those critics my only response is, "I am not a crook".)

I spent most of my 21 year Army career as a Chaplain's assistant. During that time, in '73 I married Fran and we had 3 kids (one adopted); and studied for civilian ministry through Berean School of the Bible, Springfield, Missouri. The "gospel-notes" began in about '77 as a natural outflow of military ministry & outreach to soldiers. This writing ministry & additional "notes" have continued for the 40 years since then. Most Scripture refs. are from the Revised Standard Version because that is where I started studying scripture in '72. Other versions are New American Standard, New International Version, and of course the venerable King James Version. We tend to be non-denominational, and are not endorsed by any particular group.

We have restored several homes in Oklahoma & Arizona, then got a contractor's license & built new ones. My wife and I manage & maintain rental property, which we built locally. We attend church in Cottonwood, AZ, both Protestant & occasionally Catholic.

A word about evangelism. "Evangelism is just one beggar telling another where to find bread." D.T. Niles, New York Times, May 11, 1986. "For I am not ashamed of the gospel of Christ; it is the power of God for salvation to everyone who has faith, to the Jew first and also to the Greek." Romans 1:16

* * F. J. Stone * *

My website is: www.gospelnotes.net

1
SPIRITUAL STORIES

I think of Spiritual stories as events that have happened, then reliably re-told by people of integrity. These events deal with a glimpse "beyond the physical veil" into the supernatural or spiritual dimension. These are "gifts from above" that allow us to "see" into that elusive spiritual realm. They are just sobering glimpses of things beyond.

One individual I was privileged to meet while in the military ministry was killed in a 4 fatality car wreck in Dec '04, several years after we were both out of the Army Reserve. Deceased and gone "Pastor Bill" had a close friend who came down fatally ill & passed exactly a year later, <u>on the day & hour</u> of Bill's accident. In the hospital he raised up in bed before he died & said "Why is there so much light in this room?" Actually the room was dimly lit, then he said, "You won't believe what I see over there standing alone – it's Pastor Bill!" (I hope God sends a quality reception committee for me when it's my time to go.) And for 2 other similar "stories" that are also premium glimpses of that spiritual dimension see *To Hell and Back 1993* by Maurice S. Rawlings, M.D. pages 104 & 105.

Another story is of my son when age 15 or so, who had a high-speed spill from his "big wheel" motor bike near Sedona, AZ. He came in all shaken and said, "<u>God has performed a miracle</u>. I crashed badly on a dirt trail at top speed. While flying thru the air it was like I was in a bubble in slow motion. Rocks all around but missed them all & didn't get a scratch." That happened in the spring of '92. Karl is still living the Christian life.

Then here is a "Spiritual Story" from Billy Graham's book *Angels – God's Secret Agents*, 1975 pg. 16. "A celebrated Philadelphia neurologist had gone to bed after an exceptionally tiring day. Suddenly he was awakened by someone knocking on his door. Opening it he found a little girl, poorly dressed and deeply upset. She told him her mother was very sick and asked him if he would please come with her. It was a bitterly cold, snowy night, but though he was bone tired, the doctor dressed and followed the girl. As the Reader's Digest reports the story, he found the mother desperately ill with pneumonia. After arranging for medical care, he complimented the sick woman on the intelligence and persistence of her little daughter. The woman looked at him strangely and then said, "My daughter died a month ago."

These glimpses of things beyond may be "tough to believe" (Note 175), but I personally have no problem believing these stories BECAUSE 1) Why would people lie about this kind of stuff? 2) My experience with the Gospel & Faith has been studded all along (for nearly 50 years) with glimpses of that other dimension (see link 33). And that's "why I write" gospel-notes (Note 158). While I don't consider myself to be a standard religious man, I hope to promote spirituality in Christ – it's a lifestyle & experience we can have after our decision & resolve for Christ. Once the "ice" is broken, and we learn some "principles of faith", (Note 180), spiritual stuff just happens. (And WHY there is angelic deliverance for some and not for others is truly a mystery.) Some refs. that may apply:

- Psalms 34:7 "The angel of the Lord encamps around those who fear him, and delivers them."
- Psalms 96:3-5 KJV "Declare his glory among the heathen, his wonders among all people. For the Lord is great, and greatly to be praised: he is to be feared above all gods. For all the gods of the nations are idols: but the Lord made the heavens."
- Hebrews 1:14 "Are they not all ministering spirits sent forth to serve, for the sake of those who are to obtain salvation?" (N.T. definition of angels.)
- Hebrews 13:8 "Jesus Christ is the same yesterday and today and forever."
- Revelation 3:20 "Behold, I stand at the door and knock; if anyone hears my voice and opens the door, I will come in to him and eat with him, and he with me." (Words of the resurrected J.C.)

Choose Jesus, He is Alive. And He is able to make "Spiritual Stories" with you & yours in them– it's been that way with me & mine for nearly 50 years now.

2

WORDS TO MYSELF-40 YEARS AGO

If I could go back in time to that wonderful young age of about 16 and grab myself by the neck & shake the head till the eyeballs bugged out, these are the things I would say to young Fred! Of course it would have only been "one small step for mankind, but a giant leap for me." (If I had listened.)

1. Stay away from drugs & alcohol. We are creatures of habit & it's too easy to become addicted. Fall into good habits not bad ones, ". . . your adversary the devil prowls around like a lion seeking someone to devour." 1 Peter 5:8
2. Treat your first love with respect. It is precious & fragile & if you mess it up carelessly you might hurt yourself & her long term. Song of Solomon 8:4 & 6
3. Honor your father & mother. They might be your best friends on this planet & you will miss them when they are gone. Exodus 20:5
4. Take your education seriously Fred & stay in school as long as possible. You will need it wherever you go in this hard competitive world. See Proverbs 1:20-26
5. Don't waste too much time & money (& gas) on hot rods. If you want to learn automotive, take some school classes & get credit for it.
6. Don't hasten to join the Army so you can do something exciting like shooting Asian people from a helicopter door. Life is too short to jeopardize your own donkey even if he is young & unwise.
7. Don't reject God or His values while you are young. They are both there to help you survive & get ahead in this world. Learn to pray - it greases the gears of life like nothing else. And fortunately God is totally impartial to all. He won't hear Billy Graham or the Pope sooner than you.
8. Don't ever make fun of anyone who appears to be challenged in any way. Help them if you can. God has a strange sense of justice & He may visit you with their affliction & then what will you do? (I have seen this happen, thankfully not to me.)
9. Have a little style & culture. Aspiring to be a redneck bohemian is a cheap shot. Aim for decency, truth & integrity. Those are the things that bring long-lasting satisfaction & success.

10. Fred, you should learn to think & communicate clearly. Get a mentor & discuss life's main issues. Be a little bit philosophical & ask big questions once in a while. Such as "Do good guys really come in last?"
11. Be especially careful with love & money. Losing either will be especially gut wrenching.
12. Life is what happens while you are planning something else. Don't dwell too much on the future. Have a plan, but live in the present
13. Be Christian and go to church. While there Fred, listen & think. The whole program is for your benefit. If it is any kind of a restraint on your young donkey, it's a good restraint that you need. You will meet good people there that are worth knowing.

If I had heeded my own advice, my younger years would have been more enjoyable with less painful & stupid mistakes. I did get a complete heart & soul overhaul at age 20 by accepting Christ's salvation. But from 16 to 20 was a losing devil at the wheel era in my life. At least three times death came too close. Since Jesus came in things have been altogether different & blessed. Too bad I had to learn the above "13 steps to common sense" the hard way.

3
WRESTLING WITH GOD

Webster defines wrestle as - "to struggle hand to hand with an opponent in an attempt to throw or force him to the ground without throwing blows; to struggle in opposition, strive, contend." Along with lots of other interesting stories in Genesis sure enough, we have this case of a man – Jacob – wrestling with the Divine Being in the form of a man (preincarnate J. C.?) 32:24. "Jacob was left alone; and a Man wrestled with him until the breaking of day ... v.26 and He said, let me go, for day breaks. But Jacob said, "I will not let You go unless You bless me!" Now I want to believe this was a friendly sort of opposition, and not anything like today's WWE camera - conscious "gorillas" in theatrical altercations for large quantities of money ...

Is the real purpose of all "wrestling with God" only to reach a knowledge of God and his power in one's life, AND to receive the Divine Blessing from Him? Too often today it appears that religion is mostly a matter of finding a club of clean living people to call one's own group. Of course, there is always a code of conduct, doctrine, and a meeting place on Sunday mornings which are good things. But it appears that the commitment & intensity & determination - (wrestling) - to receive from God is often missing. Did God intend for His churches to be a social operation for people who like to be around lots of other people? Then too often there seems to be an imbalance on the very nature of God. Some practically reject the Father emphasizing the Spirit. Some practically reject the Son emphasizing the Father. Some practically reject the Spirit emphasizing the Son. (If I was to choose one error above the others, it would be emphasizing the Spirit – this is His dispensation, but a balance is always good.)

Now even though God is a big dude, wrestling with Him is not like wrestling with a gorilla. God is a spirit and dealing with him is a spiritual discipline. And it is a CHALLENGE to think on things positive & Divine in this world where there are so many sinful distractions, AND human nature is so self centered. (See Colossians 3:2) Considering Jesus, meditating on his Words, solitude/quietness, ruminating on Bible concepts, and feeling for the presence of the Holy Spirit, may not at first seem to be the "rational" thing to do. But in the long run they canbecome the "treasure hidden in a field" - Matthew 13:44. Some 2600 years ago the prophet Jeremiah, said

"You will seek me and find me; when you seek me with all your heart." That's a kind of wrestling . . . (And it doesn't only have to be done Sunday mornings in church clothes.)

Another kind of wrestling is with unbelief. (See Note 17 "Concerning Quicksand") After the resurrection of Christ he appeared to the disciples, but a character named Thomas was not with them. Later he was told "we have seen the Lord" John 20:25. Then Thomas got pig headed and revealed the extent of his unbelief. (v. 25b) Eight days later all the disciples including the doubter were together & Jesus walked thru the wall and directly dealt with Thomas's doubt (v. 26-27). Then being in the presence of a living Jesus and seeing & smelling the fresh wounds of execution, Thomas replied, "My Lord and my God" (v. 28). I would say Thomas lost that "wrestling match". . . To summarize the whole thing - "Kiss the son (let Him win), lest He be angry, and you perish in the way, when his wrath is kindled but a little. <u>Blessed</u> are all those who put their trust in Him." Psalm 2:12 KJV Choose Jesus – He is Alive. Also see Note 28 "What's in it For Me?" for a look at what that blessing amounts to.

4

HOUSE PLANTS

It seems as if the last 20 years or so have seen a return of the house plant. Many folks get involved so much that these plants become a hobby. It's no wonder since living plants can be so attractive, and add that little "something" that helps to make a house a home. Now, these domesticated weeds come in all sorts, sizes, and colors. They are not abused with poison, but treated with "tender loving care." Careful watering, plant food, shining leaves, and placing in special areas, like the parlor, is part of many house plant's portion in life. Unfortunately, some refuse to live and just die, in spite of all the care they receive.

Some might laugh at the idea, but God also has a "hobby" of keeping house plants. The connection is clear that this world is His house, and we are the plants. This earth would only be a rock and not a "home" without us "plants" around. We come in all sorts, sizes, and colors; but honestly, we are basically just weeds since "all have sinned, and come short of the glory of God." (Romans 3:23 KJV). The Lord is careful not to poison the "plants" though. He "waters" them: "Whoever drinks of the water that I shall give him shall never thirst: but the water (the Holy Spirit) that I shall give him shall become in him a well of water, springing up to eternal life." (John 4:14 KJV). He "feeds" them: "He will feed his flock like a shepherd . . ." (Isaiah 40:11). He "shines" them: "Look to him (Jesus Christ), and be radiant; so your faces shall never be ashamed." (Psalms 34:5). Some are promoted to the "parlor" (heaven): "In my Father's house are many mansions: if it were not so, I would have told you. I go to prepare a place for you. And if I go and prepare a place for you, I will come again, and receive you unto myself; that where I am, there ye may be also." (John 14:2-3 KJV). Unfortunately, some wither and die, in spite of all
the provisions and care God has made for them.

My friend, as one of God's "plants", are you a weed and destined to this end: "at harvest time I will tell the reapers, gather the weeds first and bind them in bundles to be burned . . ." (Matthew 13:30). Or are you receiving His best care, and heading for the glorious supernatural "parlor" called heaven? This latter estate can really be yours - it's so simple to become a Christian. It's just a matter of admitting and confessing our sin (which we are all born into), and asking Jesus Christ to come into our life.

"If you confess with your lips that Jesus is Lord and believe in your heart that God raised him from the dead, you will be saved. For man believes with his heart and so is justified, and he confesses with his lips and so is saved." (Romans 10:9-10). ". . . and him that cometh to me I will in no wise cast out." (John 6:37 KJV). Why not take advantage of these divine provisions and become a special "house plant" destined for ultimate greatness? "... and thou shalt be like a watered garden, and like a spring of water, whose waters fail not." (Isaiah 58:11 KJV). Choose Jesus, He is Alive.

5

CROWDED CITIES

Pushing, shoving, and a general air of discontent with having so many others around is typical of the crowded city. With the heat and smoky air people also become irritable, and violence breaks out as a common occurrence. Fresh drinking water would surely help sooth frayed nerves, but congestion demands that jammed city dwellers settle for recycled water. To add to the tension, some crowded cities seem to attract all races, and problems from racial mixing develop. The general condition that results is an ugly lack of peace and love among fellow creatures of the same species.

The city of the damned will certainly be jammed (Matthew 7), and pushing, shoving, and discontent will surely be typical there also. With the heat and smoke billowing up around all souls, there will be irritation and violence in plenty. Many of the lost will cry out for water of any kind (fresh or not), but to their dismay it will be denied them (Luke 16). Fortunately, man's nature of making a negative issue of racial differences will be no problem. The total darkness in hell will prevent anyone from noticing anything about their fellow lost souls. The general condition of the crowded city below will become a burning, turbulent, rolling mass of screaming, cursing, and hatred filled souls hopelessly lost in outer darkness. Indeed, there will be a distinct lack of peace and love there.

Now the present generation has achieved a high educational level which makes many people doubt the existence of the crowded city called hell. Belief in hell is commonly ranked with belief in the tooth fairy and leprechauns. However the place is discounted and ridiculed, its <u>veracity does rest upon the words of Jesus Christ</u>. He spoke of hell (and heaven) in "no uncertain terms." Christ was a historic person as even secular and atheistic historians reveal. Therefore, the existence of hell ultimately rests upon the integrity of Jesus Christ. As the Jewish Messiah and revealed God-man of all ages, did He tell lies or the truth? To deny hell is to bash our Lord's sincerity, AND the veracity of the Scriptures.

> a) Isaiah 33:14 "The sinners in Zion are afraid; trembling has seized the godless: "Who among us can dwell with the devouring fire? Who among us can dwell with everlasting burnings?"

b)Matthew 10:28 "Do not fear those who kill the body but cannot kill the soul; rather fear him who can destroy both soul and body in hell." Jesus Christ said that.

c)Mark 9:43 "... it is better for you to enter life maimed than with two hands to go to hell, to the unquenchable fire." Jesus Christ said that.

d)Luke 16:24 (the lost) called out, "... I am in anguish in this flame."

* No one makes an honest case for the Gospel without presenting the Biblical hell.

The fact of people being crowded into cities is indeed a distressing fact of life. Even more distressing is the idea of those same unfortunate souls being assigned to an infinitely worse crowded city called hell. Fortunately, each and every person has the opportunity to improve his or her destiny through faith in and obedience to Christ. Admittedly, the fear of hell probably moves only a few toward salvation, but each soul is worth more than the world. To sum up, it should be said that if any person <u>dislikes crowded cities,</u> he should <u>avoid hell at all costs</u>. "Kiss the Son, lest he be angry, and ye perish from the way, when his wrath is kindled but a little. Blessed are all they that put their trust in him" (Psalms 2:12 KJV). Choose Jesus he is Alive, and be blessed.

6
IS THAT A CRUTCH?

The crutch is for wounded people who limp along propped up with an adjustable stick with cushioned pads for the armpit. It seems that Christian people who like their relationship with God get accused of needing a "crutch". I suppose those young Christian souls in the service or in jail get even more criticism implying they are wounded, weak & wobbly, etc.

But wait, aren't we all wounded with sin & dying an inch at a time? Sure enough that is what the Bible tells us (Romans 3:23 KJV). "For all have sinned and come short of the glory of God" (Romans 6:23 KJV). "For the wages of sin is death, but the free gift of God is eternal life in Christ Jesus the Lord". Christ comes along and offers the world & individual sinners free salvation; but too often people don't want help with life thinking they are tough, strong, self sufficient & certainly don't want a wobbly "crutch" image.

Well how about a hypothetical situation of a man who is 100 miles out in the ocean treading water, the boat sank and its gone. The water is not too cold - the sun not too hot & he is young & strong. Jesus comes along walking on the water and looks at this man and says, My son, you can't save yourself and there may be sharks out here. How long do you think you can tread water? Mr. Boat-less says, "I'm tough & strong & self sufficient - I think about 2 days". Jesus says O.K., I'll help you when you're ready. But at the end of a few hours Mr. Boat-less gets smarter & reaches up for the hand of the Lord.

> "There's a Man among us named Jesus.
> Wherever we are, he sees us.
> If in need of a hand, he's ready to stand.
> If only we ask, He frees us".*

(From the sea of despair up to the warmth of God's blessing.) "For the law of the Spirit of life in Christ Jesus has set me free from the law of sin & death" (Romans 8:2).

The "crutch" accusation for Christians has been around a long time. So have other forms of persecution & rejection (2 Timothy 3:12). But my experience with Christ & his blessing make it all worthwhile even if some think we're just weak. The salvation package He offers in this life is fabulous & it leads to eternal life in a place called Heaven. I only wish I had reached up for Jesus Christ earlier - maybe age 7 instead of 20. (See Matthew 13:44). Some old dead preacher once said, "He who has Christ as friend has an Almighty friend". (J.C. Ryle 1816-1900, Ryle's Expository Thoughts on the Gospels) And that ain't bad even if some call it a "crutch". Choose Jesus - He is Alive. See also "What's In It For Me?" Note 28.

*Poem my Fred Stone Jr.

7
I SAW THE KING

This message was originally titled "Who Is The Right One?"; it was penned in 2009. And this is a question that has been asked in many ways by millions of people for thousands of years. It can be a political question or a religious question; but history is the record of how people & nations have dealt with the question and the consequences of their answer.

The writer of this, thought Jesus Christ was probably the "right one" and made a commitment to follow Him in '72. It was an amazing journey with no disappointments, but in '77 in a spiritual dream (Joel 2:28) Jesus identified Himself in no uncertain terms. In the middle of an ordinary night while we were living in Key West, Florida there was an understanding in my mind that I was going to see Jesus. I traveled a long distance, I don't know how but the understanding or theme of the dream didn't change. I came to a large park and was walking through when I came to an old style arched footbridge. At the top of the rise I was <u>transfixed</u> due to the sight before me. There were three men in white robes on a small plaza - the size of a tennis court maybe. The man in the middle was VERY unique from the other two. I knew from instinct it was Jesus Christ. He had presence & bearing beyond ANY man of this planet. Prototype man? He seemed larger than the other two. Over his white robe was a golden brown vest made of an animal skin hair side out. It was bold & beautiful. His face was absolutely horrible due to <u>large and numerous</u> disfiguring scars but there was a glow about the scars. His hair was striking beyond words. It stood up & out like an afro, or the mane of a lion, but bolder maybe due to the silver grey color.

After a few seconds of beholding this sober scene, He turned somewhat & looked straight at me. His gaze was penetrating like the gaze of your mother, that unconditional love look – knowing all your faults. He spoke <u>three words only</u> – "LEARN OF ME." That voice was the voice of God. If I ever had any doubt of the godhood of Christ that voice cleared away all doubts. (See Psalm 29)

So "Who is the right one" - for me there is no doubt it's Jesus Christ. Interesting enough, in my dream <u>He quoted from the New Testament.</u>

Matthew 11:29 KJV - "Take my yoke upon you, and LEARN OF ME; for I am meek and lowly in heart; and ye shall find rest unto your souls." In another place He says, "I am the way, & the truth, & the life; no one comes to the Father, but by me" (John 14:6). If we are looking for the "right one" & the "right way", following Christ is the answer. There may be a lot of political & religious confusion, but that is exactly why Jesus came to the world the way he did.

He is truly the King of the universe & He has the power to come to each person as an individual. He will come to you if you want Him to. Choose Jesus - He is Alive. See also Isaiah 6:5, 9:6, 52:13-15. See also "Divine Dreams" Note 174 and "Was Jesus God?" Note 97.

Many other titles: www.gospelnotes.net

8

ELUSIVE THINGS

Elusive by definition means to avoid or escape from; hard to grasp or retain. It means to get away. Catching birds or lizards may be an elusive game. Some old country song had these lyrics - "Saw a dollar yesterday, but the wind blew it away." ("Houston", Dean Martin) Another old song of the late century had these lyrics - "Slip Sliding Away." (Paul Simon) Well, is the fabric of this world elusive by nature? Just look at the list below:

- Love & friendship. Ever lose a lover or a good friend?
- Family harmony. You may have it for a while but then your kids will become teenagers.
- Money. Ever had a shortage of the green stuff? (Do dogs have 4 feet and a tail and eat dog cookies?)
- Happiness. This is an art and a delicate balance. The demons of hell look for it & try their best to kill it.
- Sleep. Lay in the sack & not sleep all night - sometimes sleep is the most elusive.
- Peace & Quiet. Doomed on this planet. If you find it, someone will come along with a boom-box or chain saw & assassinate your P & Q post haste.
- Freedom. Ask any person in jail if freedom isn't elusive.
- Truth & Justice. Remember the most famous slam against truth ever - "What is truth?" (Pilate).
- If God in the flesh can come up short of truth & justice, the rest of us are in trouble for sure – especially in the state of Arizona.
- Youth & beauty. Every morning I look in the mirror & say, "this is not my life. Where did that old wobbly guy come from?"
- Ambition & goals & energy. "Slip sliding away."
- Optimism. The power of positive thinking might need some help at times.
- Health. Why are doctors wealthy? Because health is elusive & people are willing to pay a lot to hang on to it. (Question is, do they get their $ worth? - they still grow old and die.)
- Time. This one is like money - hard to hold on to, and it goes faster all the time.
- Ethical integrity. "All have sinned and come short. . . " (Paul the Apostle)

The things above are exactly what we live for but they are elusive. What can we do about it? Lose hope or sanity? Go on a fling? Jump off a bridge? Unfortunately, People do respond in those ways too often. Could it be that the elusive things of this world are planned that way? Is <u>the purpose of life</u> to reduce us down to a position of weakness and a lack of glamour or impressive image? Is our pride and success not really compatible with our eternal destiny anyway?

I believe life is a transition process - going from one phase to the next and generally dealing with challenges. And in spite of all the elusive things we live with, our souls can do well. Some have said "its religion when I die." I say the best approach is to catch the Spirit while young and tap into God's blessing and presence early. (See Note 28 "What's in it for me?") Connect with Christ today and let someone else fret about the elusive. Grow old in style and pass into God's best kingdom where nothing is elusive. For a picture of it see Revelation 21 & 22.

- "He made from one every nation of men to live on all the face of the earth, having determined allotted periods and the boundaries of their habitation, <u>that they should seek God</u>, in the hope that they might feel after him and find him" (Acts 17:26-27).
- "I have been young, and now am old; yet have I not seen the righteous forsaken, nor his seed begging bread" (Psalm 37:25 KJV).
- "Take delight in the Lord, and he will give you the desires of your heart" (Psalm 37:4).
- "Behold now is the acceptable time; behold, now is the day of salvation" (2 Corinthians 6:2).

Choose Jesus - He is Alive. And be blessed in spite of elusive things.

9

SERVING GOD

An ancient Hebrew prophet once said "Then shall ye return and discern between the righteous and the wicked, between him that serveth God, and Him that serveth Him not" (Malachi 3:18 KJV). This would appear to be God's basic definition of the righteous and the wicked. Another Hebrew of old was referred to as lacking – this one a king, "and he did evil, for he did not set his heart to seek the Lord" (2 Chronicles 12:14). If the purpose of life is to find God and be absorbed into eternity in style, then we are missing the boat in this country. We have become a hedonistic nation (living for pleasure and self interest). Shame on us – we need a different focus.

So what does it mean to serve or seek God? First it means accepting Jesus Christ as one's Lord and Savior. Believing in (accepting) J.C. puts us on track w/the value system of God. Today with so much atheism & alternate concepts of God, belief in the Christ of the gospels is fundamental to serving God. Jesus Himself put it this way, "This is the work of God, that you believe on him whom (God) hath sent" (John 6:29 KJV). We should also demonstrate our faith by SERVICE. James, the apostle and brother of Christ said, "so faith by itself, if it has no works, is dead" (James 2:17). And dead faith may not be any better than a dead car. You can get in it, but it won't go anywhere. We need to balance our faith with service, if God is watching us and expecting something – which He surely is.

So what kind of service? At least five things. 1) Keep His commandments. "And by this we may be sure that we know Him, if we keep His commandments. . ." (1 John 2:3). There are eleven basic ones. The ten of Moses, Exodus 20, and the one Jesus added, ". . . that you love one another" (John 15:12). That LOVE is especially needful today because it appears American people are so prone to EAT each other - see Note 29. 2) Study your Bible. "Study to show thyself approved unto God, a workman that needeth not to be ashamed . . ." (2 Tim 2:15 KJV). "Thy word is very pure; therefore, thy servant loveth it" (Psalm 119:140 KJV). Our love for God is made evident by our love of God's Word. 3) Pray. "The eyes of the Lord are upon the righteous, and his ears are open to their prayer . . ." (1 Peter 3:12). 4) Attend church at least on Sunday. This is the fourth commandment. So which church? Just pick one. If those folks are unfriendly or spiritually dead, go to the next one down the street. See

"Which Church Is Right, Note 49. 5) Then there is charitable giving to His cause. Jesus taught, "Give and it will be given to you, good measure, pressed down, shaken together, and running over, will be put into your lap. For the measure you give will be the measure you get back" (Luke 6:38), and "each one must do as he has made up his mind, not reluctantly or under compulsion . . ." (2 Corinthians 9:7). The writer, has found that giving to God's cause is better than investing with a solid bank – it's on the record and it does come back, according to our faithfulness. See "Christian Giving" Note 30.

      Much more could be said about serving God, but perhaps the high points have been touched. In conclusion: We cannot earn our way into heaven, but once our name is in the Book of Life (Rev 20:11-15), we are expected to "serve". "If any one serves me, he must follow me; and where I am, there shall my servant be also; if any one serves me, the Father will honor him" (John 12:26). Are you serving & pursuing Christ and fulfilling your purpose of being created? Or are you just hedonistic & self actualized and blowing His blessing on earth and eternity in Heaven? We all decide the way we will go. Choose Jesus, He is Alive.

10

WHAT ABOUT THE FRUIT?

Most people seem to like fruit - it looks good, feels good, smells good, tastes good. It's just a good thing to eat. Well on a higher level how does it relate to life? Especially the religious life that many people are interested in. Could it be said that anyone's faith whether Catholic, Protestant, Jewish or even Muslim consists of 3 parts: what's inside the soul, what's outside the soul, and the final destiny of the soul? Something like a threefold cord or rope which is supposed to be strong.

Final destiny part - All faiths want to believe there is a heaven or some premium future reward for living "right". Jews & Muslims value this final concept: "Fear God & keep his commandments; for this is the whole duty of man. For God will bring every deed into judgment. . ." (Ecclesiastes 12:13-14). Christian's final concept or destiny is summed up in 2 Corinthians 5:10, "For we must all appear before the judgment seat of Christ, so that each one may receive good or evil, according to what he has done in the body." Eternal rewards or losses are involved.

Outside the soul part - All faiths want to believe there are reasons or benefits of living "right". Such as: release from dark powers, free salvation, divine guidance, answered prayer, divine healing, the Church, etc. (see "What's in it for Me?" Note 28). And there should be some good stuff in our lives if we claim to be "right", or in God's family, or born again, or Christian, or whatever. Now "What About the Fruit"?

The fruit of the spirit is the Inside the soul part. And the "fruit" flows out from within. The best list I know of is this: "the fruit of the Spirit is LOVE, joy, peace, patience, kindness, goodness, faith, gentleness, self-control" (Galatians 5:22-23). In a profound respect these things "look" good, "feel" good, "smell" good and even "taste" good in our lives. What are we living for if our lives (and souls) are lacking these "fruits"? Is our faith just a dead social pattern "having the form of godliness but lacking the power thereof" (2 Timothy 3:5 KJV)? Jesus said "you will know them by their fruits". . . (Matthew 7:16), and it is possible for "bad fruit" to flow out of the soul. Such as "immorality, idolatry, sorcery, enmity, strife, jealousy, anger, selfishness, envy, drunkenness, carousing," etc. (Galatians 5:20-21).

This message is about good "fruit", but it is also about the Spirit of God. It seems that in order to have a well-balanced three part experience with God and produce good fruit we need to have His Spirit within. Christians believe that being born again comes from asking Christ to come in to our lives (Rev 3:20). Christ also encourages us to ask for the Holy Spirit (Luke 11:13). I believe the Holy Spirit is the active presence of God in our lives and that He is compatible with almost any faith that is Biblical. So if we want the good fruit we should welcome the Holy Spirit. It's sad that so many so-called Christians and churches reject the Holy Spirit and live a religious life that is out of balance. Having only the final destiny part and fire insurance is good but why cheat ourselves out of the "goodies" God has for us while we pass thru this world? Sure - some charismatic churches go to extremes in their efforts to bring down the "Spirit", but that is no excuse to "throw out the baby with the bathwater." Choose Jesus and His Spirit - THEY are Alive.

11

SOME GOOD DOPE

"The heads are together, the tea is abrew; light up the party, and pass me one too." (Anon.) This seems to be one of the more popular sentiments these days. And the curious, adventuresome nature of man does appreciate the way the wonder weed (and other varieties) affects his or her mind. The greater awareness, sensitivity, and peace make the ordinary details and experiences of life extraordinary and fun even. Time is different and everything seems to be in slow-motion except the smoker. Friendships seem better and conversation comes easier. Riding a bicycle, driving a car, or even just walking along are special and involving pastimes. Then music seems so much better - everything comes out. Now even though the whole act is temporary and <u>basically a lie</u>, the general attitude toward smoking some good dope is, "don't Bogart that joint my friend, pass it over to me." (Anon.)

Since the "Age of Aquarius" has dawned, it's a pity that so many settle for the artificial highs. It's a fact that knowing God's Spirit is very similar in many respects to being "stoned." This quality "high" enters one's being and gives him greater awareness, sensitivity, and peace. His eyes are opened to realities never imagined before. Then the ordinary becomes extraordinary as he sees dynamic divine response to the details of his daily life. The idea of God Almighty hearing and doing special things just for him is overwhelming. Receiving a needed item, job, problem solution, healing, etc. at the precise time is impressive to say the least. Realizing mysterious guidance during and after events transpire makes him wonder what the whole thing will come to. Then the general presence of the Spirit gives assurance that all is well in spite of Hell. After a while the general attitude toward this experience is "don't bogart <u>that Book</u> my friend, pass it over to me!"

Why settle for a second-rate high (especially one that's <u>demonic</u> and destructive to body, mind, and spirit) when the Majestic Power of eternity offers the best one for free? "It shall come to pass afterward, that I will pour out my Spirit on all flesh. . ." (Joel 2:28). Since He is pouring out His Spirit these last days, why not get in on it? "Do not get drunk with wine (or dope for that matter), for that is <u>dissipation</u>, but be filled with the

Spirit" (Ephesians 5:18 KJV). "Thou wilt show me the path of life: in thy presence is fullness of joy; at thy right hand there are pleasures for evermore" (Psalms 16:11 KJV). God's Spirit and Word are some good dope indeed. It's cheaper, it's deeper, more satisfying too; why not try Jesus, He's waiting for you. "Behold, I stand at the door and knock; if any one hears my voice and opens the door, I will come in to him and eat with him, and he with me." (Revelation 3: 20). Choose Jesus, He is Alive.

12

SEVEN WONDERS OF HEAVEN

When we consider the typical condition of man on this planet; carnal pride, religious pride, self sufficient, bound by various worldly habits, profane, bruised and wounded by sin, it's a "wonder" anyone gets to heaven. Then a lot of folks "wonder" if there really is such a place. But the Blood and Words of Jesus Christ can and will pave the way (Revelation 1:5 & 6). And I'm sure there are more than seven wonders of heaven, but for this page only seven.

1. The best of God's creative handy-work will be there. This world may have beauty & majesty in places but heaven outshines and surpasses this planet like comparing Disneyland with a sewer treatment plant. See 1 Corinthians 2:9

2. There cannot be any money worries in heaven. This world is racked by terrible poverty, and by the contrast of the rich having far too much. Some are starving slaves while others live like kings. This has to be repulsive to God. Maybe that's why the streets of heaven are paved with gold & the foundation stones of the city are rare jewels. And then gates of pearl of course. Revelation 21:19-21).

3. There cannot be any medical problems there. This world is replete with physical suffering & frustration. All of my mother's adult life she was crippled with a stiff leg & arthritis and medical care took most of her income (Mark 5:25-26). I "saw" her in a spiritual dream 2 years after she died & she walked normal with youthful vigor.

4. There cannot be any prideful or status conscious attitudes there. This world has a monopoly on that stuff. And the ego boosting, lying, stealing, wounding, killing, self-aggrandizing "humanness" that we all see too much of here will be completely absent from heaven. Christ's business here is to transform & clean us up so we can be received into a clean heaven and not spoil it.

5. No unresolved issues of the earthly life will carry on there. Failed love, terrible regrets, enormous guilt from one's misguided actions, anger at God for being born lame or blind, etc, etc. will not spoil anyone's joy in heaven. While I expect to have some of my life experience memories there (some of which might not be conducive to heavenly bliss), God has the provision there to sooth & heal all forms of bad memories. How about the trees of life & 12 kinds of fruit mentioned in Revelation chapter 22, "and

the leaves for the healing of nations." I can imagine being in heaven & by surprise meeting someone who ripped me off real bad (or vice versa). I will say "lets you & me go over there to that beautiful shining fruit tree and eat some leaves together for therapy." And the raunchy issues between us will be divinely healed forever.

6. No spiritual adversary there "prowling around like a lion (or snake) seeking someone to devour" (and/or possess.) See 1 Peter 5:8, Revelation 20.

7. Last but not least, seeing Jesus Christ & Biblical characters & redeemed people of this world will be awesome and wonderful. What a trip.

Well, a message like this could not have a finer ending than the words of Christ himself. (John 14:1-6 KJV) says, "Let not your heart be troubled; ye believe in God, believe also in me. In my Father's house are many mansions; if it were not so, I would have told you. I go to prepare a place for you. And if I go and prepare a place for you, I will come again and will receive you unto myself, that where I am, there ye may be also. And whither I go ye know, and the way ye know." Thomas saith unto him, "Lord, we know not whither thou goest; and how can we know the way?" Jesus saith unto him, "I am the way, the truth, and the life: no man cometh unto the Father, but by me." Choose Jesus, he is Alive. And look forward to heaven and be blessed on the way.

13

THE GOPHER

Anyone who has a lawn to care for understands the gopher problem. And it seems that the better you like your landscaping, the more sure Mr. Gopher will move in. At first a pile or two of fresh dirt here & there, then more of them. They undermine sidewalks, patios, and eat the roots of fruit trees, etc. One of the bigger challenges of these little bostids (eastern accent there) is you never see them. They are just present and very destructive, then they MULTIPLY . . .

There are a few methods of getting rid of them: traps, poison, sulfur bombs, (I used a live 5' snake once), auto exhaust and moth balls to put a bad fragrance in their tunnels. But the surest & most effective method is the surplus Russian atomic bomb. (The nuke job is only to joke about – highly illegal to perform & the collateral damage is out of the question.)

The silliness above does illustrate a truth we have to live with. The "lawn" is our world & it has a similar "gopher" that undermines & makes a mess of the whole picture. Our families mysteriously develop problems – quarreling, jealousy, anger, selfishness, etc. There will be alcoholism, gay tendencies, and devious habits of all sorts. Disappointments & failures, incarcerations, unnecessary accidents, and marriage failures are all too common. Then on the city/state level there are robberies, shootings, pimping, reckless accidents, arson, riots, and such. On the national level we have dishonest campaigning, political dysfunction, absolute fiscal irresponsibility, assassinations, terrorism, and such. There does appear to be an organized mind which promotes & causes all the mayhem. The Bible defines this "gopher" as Lucifer, Satan, devil, evil spirit, mystery of darkness, destroyer, etc. It doesn't give an exact origin as such, but of course the "serpent" was in the garden right at the beginning of the human race. We see him dealing directly with Christ in Matthew 4, then in a dramatic interaction at the close of this age in Revelation 9-20.

I believe one of the BEST strategies of our unseen adversary is to convince people he doesn't exist. But as the property owner with a gopher problem, most folks who want to control the problem of evil should start by admitting it's real. Jesus did. The gospels are full of Christ's interaction with the "gopher (s)" – we can gain <u>much insight</u> from those stories &   the Apostles instructions also.

- John 8:44b "He was a murderer from the beginning, and has nothing to do with the truth, because there is no truth in him. When he lies, he speaks according to his own nature, for he is a liar and the father of lies." J. C.
- John 10:10 KJV "The thief (satan) cometh not, but for to steal, and to kill, and to destroy: I am come that they might have life, and that they might have it more abundantly." J. C.
- Ephesians 6:12 KJV "We wrestle not against flesh and blood, but against principalities, against powers, against the rulers of the darkness of this world, against spiritual wickedness in high places."
- Peter 5:8-9 "Be sober, be watchful. Your adversary the devil prowls around like a roaring lion, seeking someone to devour. Resist him, firm in your faith . . ."

As the gopher problem is difficult to deal with, so is the bigger problem of evil undermining & making a mess of our lives. We can't "nuke" our unseen adversary (but this is exactly what the Second Coming is all about), but we can control the problem near our doorstep. That control is through personal salvation in Christ – personal commitment, prayer, worship, fellowship, giving to the cause, etc. That salvation in effect puts "treasure" instead of a "gopher" in our lawn. "The kingdom of heaven is like treasure hidden in a field which a man found & covered up. Then in his joy he goes & sells all that he has, and buys that field." Matthew 13:44 Choose Jesus, He is Alive. See also Note 43 "The Demon," & Note 195 "Why Is There Evil?"

14

THREE KINDS OF MEN *

A lot of years ago Hollywood produced the western drama, "The Good, the Bad, and the Ugly." The movie was a world-wide hit, winning academy awards for some of its actors. Few realize it, but the great director in the sky has so designed the drama of life, that mankind consists of only three kinds of men. However, its divisions aren't simply good, bad, and ugly. They are Glorified, Redeemed, and Natural.

At the present time, the Glorified is out of this world but it is the "good" division. Its ranks are the essence of quality for sure. Those people now possess a scintillating, pure, and eternal body in a supernatural dimension of life - Heaven. "Eye hath not seen, nor ear heard, nor the heart of man conceived, what God hath prepared for those who love him," (1 Corinthians 2:9 KJV)

The ranks of the Redeemed division consist of the followers of Christ on this earth. "In whom we have redemption through his blood, the forgiveness of sins, according to the riches of his grace." (Ephesians 1:7KJV). Members of this group are "partakers of the divine nature" (2 Peter 1:4), and they "look for new heavens and a new earth, in which dwelleth righteousness" (3:13 KJV). This group can be seen as "bad" because having experience & affiliation with the true God, we must endure time in this hard & evil world. We are burned out on the dog-eat-dog, throat cutting stuff & hypocrisy which goes on all around us.

The Natural division consists of all members of the race who are living for themselves. Their interests, standards, and religion reflects man's design. It is a perilous "ugly" condition "because the carnal mind is enmity against God; for it is not subject to the law of God, neither indeed can be" (Romans 8:7-9 KJV). These folks can be promoted though - it is the very reason we are all in God's drama of life. "He made from one every nation of men to live on all the face of the earth, having determined allotted periods and the boundaries of their habitation that they should seek God, in the hope that they might feel after him, and find him" (Acts 17:26-27).

To conclude this message, it won't be asked if the reader is good, bad, or ugly. The question is whether he is Redeemed and headed for Glorification. Now some will say this is a pie-in-the-sky philosophy. They're right - it is, but it's a mighty fine pie. A guaranteed one at that! "He that spared not his own son, but delivered him up for us all, how shall he not with him also freely give us all things?" (Romans 8:32 KJV). So "be renewed in the spirit of your minds, and put on the new nature, created after the likeness of God" (Ephesians 4:23-24). Jesus Christ is the only way of redemption. Choose Jesus - He is Alive. Scriptures referred to are from RSV & KJV.

* This essay was one of the earlier "Gospelnotes" – about 1979. The analogy never did fit exactly, but recent changes 2011, seem to help.

Many Other Titles: www.gospelnotes.net

15

THE ENDORSEMENT

By definition this is a statement or advertisement of a product or person by a greater entity. As Michael Jordan endorses Nike tennis shoes. Then as applied to human endeavors we want God to endorse our efforts in playing football – Dallas Cowboys praying before the game. Some air teams ask for the divine endorsement before they race hot airplanes at Reno. (I would too – at least for the sake of safety . . .) How about the general ordering the chaplain to pray before the battle in recent wars of ours? (Generals: Washington 1775, Lee 1863, and Patton 1944 did their own praying to get the Divine endorsement.)

As applied to the individual, can we get the Divine endorsement? What about that unexplainable SOMETHING to shine down on us that brings the "win" or the "victory" more often? Now generally God is very good natured according to most church doctrine. But where is He when we need that "something". Lots of folks feel that the Divine Being AND his touch is distant & uncaring towards the details & problems of their lives.

Sin is a blocker according to scripture – "If I regard iniquity in my heart, the Lord will not hear me." (Psalms 66:18 KJV). An old dead preacher named W. Herschel Ford said, "Sin is the hardest of all masters, it promises happiness. . . and brings judgment". Biblical Christianity concludes that we need the salvation of Christ to deal with the barrier of sin between people & God's endorsement. According to scripture we need to accept His gift to come into Divine favor & be "endorsed" by God. "Neither is there salvation in any other . . ." (Acts 4:12 KJV). I believe this is the basic message of ALL Christian churches: Make a personal decision for Christ (& avoid sin), and get God's endorsement/ blessing.

Too many folks deal with problems & crisis & heartaches without end. (Exactly my experience B.C.). They think the idea of divine endorsement is just a fantasy. "God can't have pets. He loves all of us the same." (common attitude) But according to scripture He has always had friends & others, Abraham & Israel are examples of "friends." The ancient Canaanites were "others" & God ordered them to be exterminated <u>due to their sinful ways</u>. The Old Testament is loaded with this concept. Jesus Christ simplified the issue in John 15:13-14 - "Greater love has no man than this; that a man lay down his life for his friends. You are <u>my friends</u> IF you do what I command you". (For more light on this see the previous chapter 14:21). Christ wants us to be born again, and participate in God's favor. The natural human condition is without God or his endorsement <u>because of</u> the sin "blocker". It is our obligation and opportunity to change that. If people have no basic need of salvation then Christ was executed for nothing, which cannot be possible.

How to get "the endorsement" for time and eternity? Do the praying thing – "Jesus save me, I need & want your blood to cover my sin & make me NEW" (2 Corinthians 5:17). Then ask for the endorsement first thing each day. "Touch my mind, my body, my goals, lead & guide, radiate that SOMETHING down on me personally because I need it & want it". In time we are likely to see this kind of headway – "the path of the righteous is like the light of dawn, which shines brighter & brighter until full day" (Proverbs 4:18). The Christian life can be a proposition where it all comes together nicely. Choose Jesus, he is Alive. And get yourself endorsed. See also Note 20, "Set Yourself Up".

* Attributed to W. Herschel Ford (1900-1976) but may have originally been stated differently by J. C. Ryle, "Gospel of Matthew – Expository Thoughts on the Gospels"

16

SEVEN MYSTERIES OF LIFE

We've all heard of the Seven Wonders of the World. Well why can't there be seven mysteries of life? I think there are at least seven.

1. Without fangs or venom, the king snake can and will kill a rattlesnake bigger than himself, and he will eat it all at once. Amazing.

2. Newlywed couples (and others) trying passionately to make babies when that is the last thing they need.

3. Religious snake handlers in Appalachia dancing in church with vipers in hand, passing them around in a frenzy, and rarely getting bit. Unbelievable but true. (I want to see this in person but I'll sit in the back close to the door.)

4. A man marrying another man. (Women marry women too, but at least they smell better.) Either way it's a mystery.

5. People with bad life habits such as drugs, alcohol, tobacco, etc. feeding the monkeys on their backs. They should kill those rascals ASAP but they often don't.

6. Elvis now has been dead 41 years and he is making more money than ever. (How can he spend it in that small living space six feet under?

7. God visited this world personally in the form of Jesus Christ and proved himself by walking on water, raising the dead, healing blind eyes, turning water into wine (and not getting drunk), and other awesome deeds. THEN he allowed himself to be brutally murdered by his creatures to become   the Lamb of God. This has to be the most mysterious class act of all time. And we have all heard of the resurrection & ascension into heaven of Christ after He was dead 3 days. Now it's been almost two thousand years and people say He's still alive and active in this world, soon to return personally.

Well, I don't understand the first six mysteries on this page, and nobody with only human intelligence understands ≠7. But when we believe it, God has promised to open our eyes to His reality & bless us the way only He can in life and eternity. Jeremiah 29:11-12 says, "I know the plans I have for you, says the Lord, plans for welfare and not for evil, to give you a future and a hope. Then you will call upon me and come and pray to me, and I will hear you." John 3:16 - "For God so loved the world that he gave his only Son that whoever believes in him should not perish but have eternal life." Choose Jesus and His Spirit - they are Alive & mysteriously good.

17

CONCERNING QUICKSAND

The visitor to South Florida is usually impressed at the unusual plant and animal life. He sees the tropical plants of so many sorts - vines, trees, and bushes, all of which seem to grow like mad. Then there is the winged critters of all sizes and colors. He notices that monkeys also thrive there by the number of road-side ape attractions. As the South Florida region is much like a jungle, the visitors and residents should all be glad that there is no quicksand to complete the charm.

But wait! Is there no quicksand? Yes, there is. It's a variety that slowly and naturally bogs it's victims down. This "mud" at first seems harmless, but gets a strong hold on one before he knows it. Too many times it draws people into it up to their necks. During the struggle the victim realizes too late that he is almost dead with the "mud" at his head, without hope of grabbing a rope. Soon, he is gone.

Now many will not admit the danger of South Florida quicksand. But in the jungle of life, unbelief is spiritual "quicksand" and it is found anywhere we may go and is infinitely worse than regular quicksand. We are programmed from our early years to question all that God has recorded for us in the Book. Seven day creation is replaced by "monkey-business." Reincarnation and astrology effectively undermines the teachings of Christ. After this groundwork is laid, the victim's mind is programmed to reject the simple Gospel of Jesus Christ and His salvation. He is too wise to believe "all that" - especially in this age of enlightenment. He settles down in his pride, false convictions & sin while the years pass and his heart is hardened beyond the point of hope. (Note 173 "Strong Delusion") Soon, he is gone.

As the above views may be hard to swallow, let's refer to the Book. "The iniquities of the wicked ensnare him, and he is caught in the toils of his sin. He dies... he is lost." (Proverbs 5:22-23). "For God so loved the world that he gave his only Son, that whoever <u>believes</u> in him should not perish but have eternal life." (John 3:16). "Without faith it is impossible to please him: for he that cometh to God must <u>believe</u> . . ." (Hebrews 11:6 KJV). "He that overcometh shall inherit all things; and I will be his God, and he shall be my son. But the fearful, and <u>unbelieving</u>, and the abominable... shall have their part in the lake which burneth with fire and brimstone: which is the second death." (Revelation 21:7-8 KJV).

Let's not get stuck in the "quicksand" of unbelief. God has put us here to find out who will believe Him and who will not. Let's pass through this jungle and walk on top of the mud holes, water, devils (see "Mindset of Victory" Note 103) and all else that would drag us under into eternal loss of our souls. "As many as received him, to them gave He power to become the sons of God, even to them that <u>believe</u> on his name." (John 1:12 KJV). Receive Jesus Christ today and hook-up with eternity. Scriptures referred to are: RSV and KJV.

18

THE DATE

Stand up, hook up, shuffle to the door;
   jump right out & count to four.
If that chute don't open wide,
   I've got another one by my side
If that chute don't open either,
   I've got a date with old Saint Peter.   (Army Cadence rhyme)

In some military circles, this is one of the more popular thoughts about death these days. Of course, not many folks take the issue of death seriously, but since we all roll over and die eventually, let's look at it now.

There is an old book that speaks of such facts and it has a way of being "right-on" time after time. Whoever wrote it must have had his "head together" because it has even predicted the future hundreds of years in advance dozens of times. This old book also speaks much about a pretty popular character we all hear about and speak of each day. In fact, the average American male (in the service) refers to Jesus Christ about six or eight times a day. (Too bad it's in a profane way.) It is this Character, and not Saint Peter in any sense, that we have that date with when we sigh our last bad breath (or explode from hitting the landscape at 150 miles per). See John 5:22.

I am impressed that we won't recognize Him at first due to his terribly disfigured face and scarred body. The old book says "his appearance was so marred beyond human semblance, and his form beyond that of the sons of men." (Isaiah 52:14) The setting will sober us to the marrow - its vivid color, sound, and living realness beyond anything of this life. Then He will speak. His voice will resound from the ends of the universe with ultimate authority and blood curdling finality. "He reflects the glory of God and bears the very stamp of his nature, upholding the universe by his word of power." (Hebrews 1:3) Whether we are right with Him or not, truly "it is a fearful thing to fall into the hands of the living God." (Hebrews 10:31). And we will all fall into those hands. See "I Saw the King" Note 7.

At that time there will be only one thing that matters - whether we have passed the test of life or not. The grading will not be curved - <u>the cut off score</u> will be, "you rejected Jesus Christ and His salvation." Now He spoke of the loser's reward as a place of "gnashing of teeth" and "eternal fire." My friend, no one is destined to that place - it's his own personal choice. Are you making that choice? "How shall we escape, if we neglect so great salvation, which at first was spoken by the Lord, and was confirmed unto us by them that heard Him." (Hebrews 2:3 KJV)

`Let's cheat death and hell by simply aligning ourselves with that Man from Galilee who said, "I am the door; by me if any man enter in, he shall be saved, and shall go in and out, and find pasture." (John 10:9 KJV) And, "I am the way, and the truth, and the life: no one comes to the Father, but by me." (John 14:6). And when we live the Christian life, God typically blesses his redeemed people real good. See "What's In It For Me?" Note 28 Choose Jesus He is Alive.

19

SAD FACTS OF LIFE

In about 1974 an old man in Oregon told me, "Fred you will see some sad things in your life." Well I didn't know what he meant but it almost seemed like prophecy the way it came out of him. For about 35 years I have made the following observations. Many of which were learned the hard way.

- Love can & will turn into hate. Young love is especially at risk. The purpose of love is to make life better but it often backfires when people are ignorant or inexperienced with love, and don't know how to guard it.
- For some problems there is no human solution and/or human counsel.
- Too often people with many friends value each only a little. People with few friends value each too much.
- When you are down & depressed expect little help from others. Most likely you will be "kicked" and/or rejected.
- When you do your best, often it won't be appreciated or it won't be good enough.
- People generally don't care much about others (unless there is an ulterior motive.) When many friendships seem to be shallow, this may be quite normal.
- When you try real hard to get something perfect, it won't survive because something will come along and spoil it nearly every time.
- If a group leader is attractive, warm & friendly, popular, etc, then the group followers will defend him right or wrong, Truth be irrelevant.
- Humans are supposed to be better than any animal of God's creation. Often they are lower than animals. Animals respect their master or at least the one who feeds them. Humans don't always. Animals don't bomb or gas or otherwise kill masses of their own kind. They don't systematically kill their babies either. Man even killed his Creator when He came to visit. See link 182 "Human Nature".
- It's sad when you intend for something you say or do to be cute or funny, but it gets misinterpreted to be rude or spiteful. Then you end up losing friends and being public enemy number one.
- When people or an entity is given too much too regular, the gift will at some point be expected, or almost owed. At that point the giver becomes a RAT if he stops giving.

- It's sad when God's people are too competitive, i.e. holier, more spiritual, more knowledgeable, etc. but have lost sight of love.
- It's sad when God's people are too social or status conscious, but have lost sight of spirituality.
- All people wear a mask. Nobody is as fine as they wish to appear.
- The things fallen human nature needs most to elevate it are BIBLICAL TRUTH and FAITH. Those things are constantly avoided as most people lapse deeper in unbelief & sin. See Note 17 "Concerning Quicksand".
- "Truth shall forever be on the scaffold, and wrong forever on the throne - as long as time shall last." James Russell Lowel, 1819-1891
- Friendship is where you find it, not necessarily where it's supposed to be. Don't count on "given" friends such as family members, neighbors, minister, church acquaintances, etc. as they may disappoint you. See Proverbs 18:24
- Big hearted, compassionate, caring people will be exploited. Those who don't know how to say NO will be taken to the cleaners.
- People believe what they want to believe. It's sad that this human trait doesn't usually employ much reason, logic, or a careful analysis of the facts. All forms of prejudice thrive while Truth gets abused in this environment.
- If you're successful, you win false friends and make true enemies.
- Honesty and frankness will get you nowhere: They make you vulnerable.
- People really need help but they attack you if you try to help them.
- Give the world the best you have and you sometimes get kicked in the mouth. See "Hazards of Giving" Note 131.

Well, being aware of such "facts" may be helpful but it does call for a word of encouragement. If it's all true, how do we avoid becoming negative "nervous Nellies" ourselves? The Jesus of the Bible was a very special person and He said "Come to me, all you who labor and are heavy laden, and I will give you rest. Take my yoke upon you and learn from me, for I am gentle and lowly in heart, and you will find rest for your souls. "For My yoke is easy and my burden is light." (Matthew 11:28-30) When we accept Christ's salvation, and live in faith (Psalms 23) God can and will show us all kinds of neat "stuff" and give the "victory" over this world's sad facts. Isaiah put it this way; "The Lord will guide you continually, and satisfy your desire with good things, and make your bones strong; and you shall be like a watered garden, like a spring of water, whose waters fail not." (Isaiah 58:11) Choose Jesus He is Alive. See Note 157 "Happy Facts of Life".

20
SET YOURSELF UP . . .

Several years ago my passion in life was to fly airplanes. I remember those days real well, and especially some of my landings. Especially the dangerous ones. In ground school young pilots are/were taught to "set yourself up to land." This means to get in the "pattern" and follow the basic rules carefully (or exactly) and then a good landing will happen. (A monkey could do the take off with only a little help, but that monkey would sure make a big mess of the landing.) You don't sit up in the sky in an aircraft and point it at the runway below and head for the ground. That method will bust the airplane & passengers every time. Hitting the end of the runway at 150 MPH is only good for heavy airliners.

The pattern starts at about 800 ft. above the ground. The inbound to land aircraft enters the pattern about a half mile from the runway and parallel to it flying with the wind. For light aircraft maybe 80 MPH depending on type of AC. Power is then cut back & the bird will begin to descend. This is the "downwind leg" of the pattern. At about half mile beyond the end of the runway and about 600 feet above ground the pilot makes a standard 90 degree turn (left is normal) and enters the "base leg" of the pattern. The speed will be about 75 MPH. Just before reaching alignment with runway the pilot turns 90 degrees again to line up straight with the runway into the wind. This is the "final approach." Speed will be about 70 MPH and 300 ft. above ground. The pilot holds alignment and speed exactly and carefully touches down at end of runway. This pilot "set himself up to win" by observing the aviation "pattern" rules, and made a good landing.

People fail to realize that in life there is also a "pattern" that needs to be followed to "win." Such as getting a legitimate education for their intended vocation, living within their means, avoiding pitfalls like drugs & alcohol abuse, teamwork in the home, and being productive. Then God's salvation is also a big part of the "pattern" and the successful "landing." God's word tells us, "Take delight in the Lord and He will give you the desires of your heart." (Psalms 37:4) "...Stand by the roads, and look, and ask for the ancient paths, where the good way is; and walk in it, and find rest for your souls." (Jeremiah 6:16) "The Lord shall guide thee continually, and satisfy thy soul in drought, and make fat thy bones; and thou shalt be like a watered garden, and like a spring of water, whose waters fail not," (Isaiah 58:11 KJV)

The above "pattern" of successful living is greatly enhanced by living and walking with Jesus Christ. Why not tap into God's free salvation & blessing by accepting Christ today? "Behold, I stand (J.C.) at the door and knock, if anyone hears my voice and opens the door, I will come into him and eat with him and he with me." (Revelation 3:20) Don't set yourself up to lose. Choose Jesus and His spirit. And SET YOURSELF UP TO WIN. See also Note 27 "What's In It For Me?"

21
SOUL BROTHERS

The following paragraphs on this page were written in '79. But now that the U.S. has its first ever black president, this message may have come "full circle." And it does appear that we have all entered a new era as people of color represent our president each day AND as MLK himself dances in the streets of heaven.

Probably everyone is familiar with the "soul movement" to some extent. About every day we hear soul music on the radio or TV, and soul talk - jive, if you will. Soul food is a big thing. Then, there is the afro hair styles which are marvelous indeed. And of course, we have the tinted windows and low-riding in some cities. America would not be the same without soul brothers and sisters and their unique culture.

However interesting and original the soul movement is, it is surely time we realize that we've all got a claim on the act in a certain sense. Now some folks truly would have trouble sporting an afro. Some may not honestly appreciate the ham hocks and chitlins. But brother, the fact of the business is, you got a soul and I got a soul - that makes us "soul brothers." So what is a soul? It's a sad truth that too many folks just don't know.

Theologians believe each person is a three - part being; body, mind and soul. The soul is the DIVINE part and is attached to the blood. This may explain why we feel emotions (the best of humanness) in the center of our chest and not in the head. "The life of the flesh is in the blood . . ." (Leviticus 17:11) and when the blood pours out of the body, the soul returns to its maker. I believe the soul contains a divine "memory chip" that causes the NEW body & mind to be restored to the soul after death. This gives real value and potency to the lost/saved teaching of the Bible. If saved, your full awareness, personality, and mind will enjoy with others the wonder of God's supernatural city and creation in a supernatural body forever. If lost, the same resurrected YOU will be wasted forever in a place Jesus Christ called Hell.

Soul brother, what is your status right now? Are you stuck in the mire of today's unbelief and under a divine curse for time and eternity? Or are you enjoying God's very real blessings now and the fantastic and sure promise of heaven? These are heavy questions and apply to every one of us. Why not make your peace with God right now and become a soul brother in the highest sense. Heaven will not be the same without YOU. God says,

"Behold, all souls are mine . . . the soul that sinneth, it shall die." (Ezekiel 18:4 KJV) Jesus said, "I am the resurrection and the life; he who believes in me . . . shall never die." (John 11:25-26) "In my Father's house are many mansions: if it were not so, I would have told you. I go to prepare a place for you. And if I go and prepare a place for you, I will come again, and receive you unto myself; that where I am, there ye may be also." (John 14:2-3 KJV) It is hoped that this message has helped some find a living faith in Christ. If so, do get involved in a legitimate Bible-believing church where you can survive and grow as a Christian.

Over 200 other titles at www.gospelnotes.net

22

THE TAKE – OFF

You're sitting on the hold line or the numbers and clearance comes from the tower. As you push in the throttle and gain speed the feeling of victory increases. The lift off speed approaches so you pull back slightly on the control wheel. At the moment of lift off, the bird goes from a very high rolling speed to a very low flying speed. The flying speed is just above the stall point. The bird flies sluggishly and any folly or stunts could be very fatal. After the climb-out the aircraft levels off and picks up speed along with stability, control responsiveness, and mission progress.

In life it's similar. The human is ready to be born in the hospital. The time is right (even if not a big delight) and bingo - a new physical life has officially begun. It starts out slowly and gradually picks up speed. There is a general feeling of victory as the age of accountability and adulthood is reached. But the Spirit calls and the soul looks up. It enters into the new realm of Spiritual Life realizing it was made to fly. But from the point of high physical strength and progress to the level of an infant again is a shock to the individual. His spiritual stature is small, weak, ineffective, and the contrast is humiliating. His climb-out is a real challenge since the pull of gravity (sin) is strong. At this point any folly or games with God could be fatal to his spiritual headway and possibly cause a crash. As growth continues, he levels off, picks up confidence, and becomes stable, responsive to the Spirit, and mission progress begins to happen.

Wouldn't you be excited if God Himself spoke to you personally (hypothetical situation here) with a heavy voice and said, "Friend, I want to <u>save you from hell</u> and <u>adopt you</u> as my own son/daughter. <u>My Spirit will come into your being</u> and give you a new start, <u>my own perspective</u>, <u>and guide you</u> to ultimate personal fulfillment in this life and prepare <u>a place for you in celestial glory</u> to spend eternity with me." Any normal person would not only be excited but would probably pass out for joy at the offer. Well, He probably won't call you in such a dramatic way, but the offer is truly open to you right now and the promises are AT LEAST the same. However, there is one small catch. To claim God's very real gifts, you must receive Jesus Christ. Will you do it? Will you take-off today before it's too late? No one knows the length of his runway.

"Behold, I stand at the door and knock; if any one hears my voice and opens the door, I will come in to him and eat with him, and he with me." (Revelation 3:20 - Jesus Christ) "Therefore, if anyone is in Christ, he is a new creation; the old has passed away, behold, the new has come." (II Corinthians 5:17) "And the LORD shall guide thee continually, and satisfy thy soul in drought, and make fat thy bones; and thou shalt be like a watered garden, and like a spring of water, whose waters fail not." (Isaiah 58:11 KJV) "But as it is written, Eye hath not seen, nor ear heard, neither have entered into the heart of man, the things which God hath prepared for them that love him." (I Corinthians 2:9 KJV). Choose Jesus, He is Alive.

23

TO BE A MAN

This has got to be a very important issue to all people - especially males. What does it mean to be a man? Is it an attitude or achievement or lifestyle or what? Whatever it is, it churns deep in the heart or soul & comes out in various forms of I AM:

1. "I am tough & strong." At 6' and 225 lbs of muscle & coordination I am a man. (not me)
2. "I am smart." Well <u>these degree titles</u> from well known universities prove it. I am a man (not me either).
3. "I am rich & successful." Too many people want to be in this crowd & many who are say in their hearts, "I am a man" nearly all play the "I AM" game.
4. "I am an American serviceman." (Army, Navy, Marine, Air Force, etc.) The rest of you wouldn't have this good country or your freedom and you might not be speaking English without us. (And its true) They think they are classic MEN.
5. "I AM A Harley Davidson biker." We know what it means to be a man. Don't mess with us.
6. In the southwest of the U.S. we have the cowboy thing where young men ride mad 2,000 pound bulls and wild horses at rodeos to prove manhood.

This list could go on and on and it would get really strange and bizarre if we looked at other nationalities' concepts of manhood. Like Eastern Africa or Madagascar or India. And I believe God himself looks down on all these altercations with varying degrees of interest, admiration, sympathy, bewilderment, and/or sometimes disgust.

Now what would God's concept of manhood be? One could look at male Bible characters and get some ideas. Samson, Job, Moses, Elijah, David the shepherd and others, these all were different characters but they all had FAITH which they mixed with action. Stately Isaiah "cut through the chase" when he wrote God's thinking on the "man" subject, "...this is the man to whom I will look, he that is humble and contrite in spirit, and trembles at my word." Isaiah 66:2 Well <u>there in a nutshell - humble, contrite and respecting God's Word</u>, is what He wants in manhood. Jesus can be seen as the best qualities of all Bible characters that came before him. He can be followed through the gospels (Matthew, Mark, Luke & John) to see the most aggressive living example of manhood & character. <u>Jesus had it all</u>. He was strong, smart, successful if not rich, service oriented, had manly bearing, & was very scripture minded. He died humbly & bravely for his cause. Jesus was a man and as the God-man of all ages he can truly say "I AM" THE MAN. And it is a gross mistake to think that Jesus Christ is effeminate or a hippie type "person." Jesus is deity and He invented male/female gender. (Genesis 1:26-27)

The writer of this had a personal glimpse of "the man" in 1977 in a spiritual dream. See Note #7 "I Saw The King." I believe for sure if the J.C. that I saw walked into a H. D. motorcycle club, they would all get real quiet. His "manly" bearing & scars & presence would <u>overwhelm them ALL</u>. I can imagine him walking to the beer keg & turning it into holy water. At His invitation 90% of the bikers would want to follow Christ & be baptized by Him right there. And if he spoke <u>one word</u> His majestic VOICE would win the other 10%. (Psalm 29:3-9)

"What is man, that thou dost make so much of him, and that thou dost set thy mind upon him, dost visit him every morning and test him every moment?" (Job 7:17-18) Our human concepts of manhood may be OK but God's concept should also be considered. Choose Jesus He is Alive - and be a follower of THE MAN. See John 14:6, Revelation 3:20

24

WHO CAN YOU TRUST?

The question above is a valid one and it's pondered by many. Webster defines trust as, "firm belief or confidence in the honesty, integrity, reliability, justice, etc. of another person or thing." Well after more than 60 years of life experience I have much discouragement.

First, can you trust yourself? Most honest souls will say no. How about close family members. Not always - remember, the first family in this world, one brother killed the other (Cain & Able). How about the doctor? Those characters are considered professional but they have "stepped on the oath" too many times. (The whole U.S. medical/pharmaceutical industry appears to be mainly about money). How about the realtor? Too often truth is lacking here for sure. Salesmen of all kinds have a reputation for stretching and/or hiding truth. The investment advisor? No - they have been known to tell more lies than some politicians, and not be accountable for one thing they say. How about the school teacher: These days they sometimes seduce their pupils. What about commercial pilots. Chasing stewardesses & sometimes flying intoxicated - God help those who fly . . . Well preachers should be a truthful & trustable lot. Jim Jones of Guiana & his 900 plus dead followers scattered all over the ground comes to mind. I have personally known well about 20 preachers & two I strongly believe were demon possessed imposters - at least judging by their liberal theology & psychotic actions. That's 10 percent false in a class that should be 99% true. My observation or conclusion is that it's hard to trust anyone, because this earth is truly the PLANET of LIES. (And greed, and misfits, etc.)

It is interesting that the Bible says "God is not a man that he should lie, or the son of man that he should repent." (Numbers 23:19) A lot of people stay away from God because He is so righteous, but these days we need to see something or someone with GOOD character. And He is a refreshing oasis of STELLAR goodness & power. So besides being Holy, (pure & sinless) what is God like? Eternity is beyond time - He lives there. Life is an invention of God. Immutable is not able to change, (unlike us dirtbags, we change every day). Omnipotence - having all power. Omnipresent - all places at the same time. Omniscient - knowing all things. Creation is His business . . . He is the Author of Salvation. He is pleased to give Forgiveness and receive Prayer & Worship from humans. He claims to be the ultimate judge of individuals & mankind. Amazing enough the person of Jesus

Christ laid claim to ALL the above attributes during his ministry on earth. That is equality with God which is beyond awesome.

Who can you trust? I am convinced that we can believe & trust God fully. We may not always be able to trust our own kind, (especially in this age of lies & uncertainty). But the God of the Bible has demonstrated His trust-worthiness. Have you connected? If not, why not? God's salvation in Jesus Christ is available to "whosoever will". He has proven to be not only honest but also a personal healer, counselor, protector & friend for millions including myself. "Blessed is the man who makes the Lord his trust, who does not turn to the proud . . ." (Psalm 40:4) . . . "For unto us a child is born, to us a son is given; and the government will be upon his shoulder, and his name will be called Wonderful, Counselor, Mighty God, Everlasting Father, Prince of Peace." (Isaiah 9:6 KJV) "Kiss the Son, lest he be angry, and ye perish from the way, when his wrath is kindled but a little. Blessed are all they that put their trust in Him." (Psalm 2:12 KJV) Choose Jesus - He is Alive.

25

THE TALE OF TWO BETRAYALS
(or The Devil Made Me Do It)

    I know we all have had some experience with betrayal. Sometimes as the Betrayer and sometimes as the Betrayed. I think of a dark time in Jesus' Ministry when he was celebrating Passover with his disciples and he was soon to become the Passover Lamb himself. I think about Judas Iscariot and how he had spent hours, days, years at the foot of the Master, witnessing His healings, raising the dead, His casting out of demons, and numerous other miracles. He had seen Jesus' joy, anger and tears. He even had his feet washed by the Son of God. What could have turned his heart so cold? Was it an act of his will or some demonic control that was beyond his own choices? Could ever our own hearts be so stony within our chests that we could turn from our Savior and sell Him to his death for thirty pieces of silver? Perhaps an examination of the scriptures could shed some light? Jesus said "Woe to that man who betrays the Son of man. It would be better for him if he had not been born". (Matthew 26:24 KJV) Mark echoes the same words. But Luke gives us some insight into the spiritual side of the equation with "Then satan entered Judas, called Iscariot. . ." (Luke 22:3 KJV). John provides the most spiritual insight with ". . . The devil had already prompted Judas Iscariot, son of Simon, to betray Jesus" (John 13:2 KJV) and finally "as soon as Judas took the bread, satan entered into him. . ." (John 13:27 KJV). This seems to indicate that while Judas was setting up the deal with 30 pieces of silver as the prize, he was "prompted" by satan but wasn't fully taken over by him until he accepted the piece of bread that had been dipped. The bread scenario was a fulfillment of scripture according to Jesus in John 13:18 ". . . he who shares my bread has lifted up his heel against me." The prophecy coming from (Psalms 41:9 KJV) "even my close friend whom I trusted, who shared my bread, has lifted up his heel against me." Almost as if the completion of this prophecy was the signal for satan to take possession.

    Now of course, in an act of free will we also have the free will to seek forgiveness. It is said in Matthew 27:3-4 KJV when Judas, who had betrayed Him, saw that Jesus was condemned, he was seized with remorse and returned the thirty silver coins to the chief priests and elders, "I have sinned" he said "for I have betrayed innocent blood" then in verse 5 "so Judas threw the money into the temple and left. Then he went away and

hanged himself." Now on some level it would please me to think that Judas' remorse lead to his repentance and he sought forgiveness. But none of his
actions following his sorrowfulness would indicate that Judas considered himself forgiven.

I did say this was a Tale of Two Betrayals . . . The second Betrayal also happened on the same night in question. Let's go straight to the spiritual happenings as recorded in Luke 22:31-32 KJV, "Simon, Simon, satan has asked to sift you as wheat. But I have prayed for you, Simon that your faith may not fail. And when you have turned back, strengthen your brothers."

Now it is obvious that Simon Peter also witnessed the same acts of Jesus that Judas had, yet had a different impact on his life. Let's make clear that Peter was not without faults. A sense of arrogance being chief among them. In the following verse he says "Lord, I am ready to go with you to prison, and to death" (Luke 22:33). Personally, I have found that in a fight the talking part is easier than the fighting part. He denied knowing Jesus & cursed and swore to make his point. As Jesus predicted the cock crowed the third time and Peter's betrayal was complete. His response afterward, consistent in three Gospels, "he wept bitterly". Both individuals identified their mistake but their responses varied greatly from that point on. Judas went on to suicide and Peter went on to repentance and restoration and on to lead the greatest act of love God ever bestowed upon mankind. Christianity.

Any man (woman) can witness God's miracles and love and go on to betray that very same love. It is how he responds after he recognizes that sin that makes all the difference. Color that monkey any color you want, if it keeps you from God then it is sin and needs to go. Life is too short and eternity too long to delay how you will respond to Jesus' call. Sin is a spiritual sickness and needs to be dealt with in your spirit. Choose wisely, ask forgiveness, forgive yourself, and grow in God's light.

* * Andrew B. Hellman * *

26

THE UNDERDOG

What is an underdog? Is it a dog that walks under trucks (like my dog Elmo does)? Webster says originally it is "a dog that is losing in a dogfight." It is also a PERSON "who is handicapped or at a disadvantage because of injustice, discrimination, etc." How about the young soldier, the poor, the uneducated, the incarcerated, the unattractive, the addict, the abused/rejected from youth, the slave, the pessimist, the loner, the outsider, the one who asks too many questions (like me), or the person who just can't seem to get ahead. These can all be underdogs & every society has a lot of them. I've heard it said that "people favor underdogs, but they follow top dogs."

Well, if there is a just God up there, who does he "favor or follow"? Does any class of people have an advantage with God? Does He have priorities? The point of this message is this: while God is impartial to all, He does seem to identify with or even seek out the underdog. Consider such Biblical characters as Joseph, Gideon, David, Mordecai, Amos, doubting Thomas, and others. They needed and received a special touch from above. Christ's ministry while on earth focused on the poor & needy & rejected of that day. Consider the wholesale quantity of amazing miracles performed for the underdogs of Palestine in the four gospels - Matthew, Mark, Luke, and John. Then Christ himself, although he was God in the flesh, was an underdog IN THE SENSE that the religious leaders rejected him & denied him justice. "He came to his own home, and his own people received him not." (John 1:11). See also Isaiah 53:3.

Now the apostle Paul who defined much of Christianity had this to say about underdogs – ". . . not many of you were wise according to worldly standards, not many were powerful, not many were of noble birth; but <u>God chose</u> what is foolish in the world to shame the wise, <u>God chose</u> what is weak in the world to shame the strong, <u>God chose</u> what is low and despised in the world, even things that are not, to bring to nothing things that are, so that no human being might boast in the presence of God." (1 Corinthians 1:26-29) Now James, (who may have been the natural brother of Christ) said this, "Has not God chosen those who are poor in the world to be rich in faith and heirs of the kingdom . . .?" (James 2:5)

It is evident that the underdog has an advantage with God, BUT he or she still needs to activate their faith if they want to get anything from divine quarters. Such as free salvation, God's blessing, and numerous benefits, see Note 28 "What's In It For Me?" Connect with Christ today – "Behold, I stand at the door and knock, if anyone hears my voice and opens the door, I will come in to him and eat with him, and he with me." (Revelation 3:20) "Take delight in the Lord and he will give you the desires of your heart." (Psalms 37:4) "God is our refuge and strength, a very present help in trouble." (Psalms 46:1) Choose Jesus, he is Alive and loves underdogs such as myself.

27

THE WORLD

In spite of the fact that people daily relate to the world, few pause to consider what it actually is. Not only is the world our beloved environment – the earth, sky, and vegetation, but humanity and its styles, attitudes, and customs are major factors. It is the system of friends, loved ones, possessions and being at home in ones particular society. A basic natural view of the world is this. Now with a spiritual orientation the picture is considerably different.

A notable writer, H.C. Mears wrote, "The world is that system about us or that spirit within us which is blind and deaf to spiritual values and cares nothing for the will of God." Maybe that means the world has a tendency to promote self-centeredness, prideful attitudes, sometimes moral degradation. At any rate, the peaceful, conservative Spirit of Christ is not always received well `by the spirit of the world. Members of God's family are often despised, criticized, and ostracized by the world for having Christ's Spirit and values. The worldly crowd sees Christians as being strange as indeed they are "Strangers and pilgrims on the earth" (Hebrews 11:13 KJV). The epitome of the Christian Spirit, Christ himself, was crucified by the world. Christ said of his original followers "They are not of the world, even as I am not of the world" (John 17:16). There are answers to the Christian's dilemma in the old Book. Often God's people resign themselves to this attitude: "This old world's not my home, I'm just a passin through. My treasures are laid up somewhere beyond the blue . . ." And I can't feel at home in this old world anymore." Jim Reeves "This World Is Not My Home"; Sony/ATV Music Publishing LLC

Now it might be in order to include the most famous thought from the New Testament that mentions "the world." "God so loved <u>the world</u> that he gave his only Son, that whoever believes in him should not perish but have eternal life" (John 3:16). That passage speaks for itself. Then God's replacement for Judas, the amazing apostle Paul wrote this -- "Do not be conformed <u>to this world</u>, but be transformed by the renewal of your mind, that you may prove what is the will of God, what is good and acceptable and perfect" (Romans 12:2). And it wouldn't be right to omit the apostle of love in this "world" essay. John wrote, "Love not <u>the world</u>, neither the things that are in <u>the world</u> . . . the lust of the flesh, and the lust of the eyes, and the pride of life, is not of the Father, but is of <u>the world</u>" (1 John 2:15-

16).

     Even though the true Christian Spirit gets few takers in this world, it does offer more freedom to be an individual. Can you imagine not being bound by the world's styles and attitudes, and also being free of the opinion of others? Friend, is your spirit basically the same as the spirit that crucified Christ? Does the world and its god (Satan) control your life and destiny? (2 Corinthians 4:4) Solemn questions indeed; and just as valid today as when Christ discussed them nearly 2000 years ago. Freedom from the world and its spirit is possible by receiving Christ. Be Born Again and marvel at the thought, "blessed are the meek, for they shall inherit the earth" (Matthew 5:5). Choose Jesus, He is Alive.

28

WHAT'S IN IT FOR ME?

Sooner or later we all hear about God's claim on our souls & lives. Maybe from a T.V. evangelist or a religious booklet or a friend or by whatever means the message comes. Most people listen and some make a decision. But all ask the question above. And it's a legitimate question. Listed below are some of the benefits of being Christian.

1. Release from dark powers. Most folks are quick to say that's rubbish - either there is no devil or he has no power over me. . . Well according to the Bible he has a legal claim to this world and all the people in it. (The Apostle Paul's mission) ". . . to open their eyes, that they may turn from darkness to light and from the power of Satan to God. . ." (Acts 26:18) See also Matthew 4:8-9.
2. Free salvation. The scriptures talk about lost/saved issues very often, especially in the New Testament. See John 3:16 & Acts 4:12.
3. Relief from the fear of death & hell. The Bible discusses life & death issues clearly & with authority. We see who & what God is & how he is a constant factor in life while man comes & goes; <u>all of us</u>. The knowledge disclosed about the afterlife (especially for the saved) dispels uncertainty & fear of the unknown.
4. Divine guidance. This can be a direct thing from the Holy Spirit or general teaching from the Word of God. Either way it's great to be directed from a higher power rather than stumbling along "blind" & "eating" much more heart aches & troubles than we should. Then it leads us to the BEST VERSION OF OURSELVES and I believe better days. (Habakkuk 3:19) See Note 143 "Divine Guidance".
5. Answered prayer. Anyone can pray but the secret is <u>being heard & answered</u> by a Christ who knows & cares about our needs. "The eyes of the Lord are upon the righteous, and his ears are open to their prayer" . . . (1 Peter 3:12). See Note 37 "What is Prayer".
6. Divine Presence. God has always desired to be "present" with people. And Christians have access to a Counselor/Comforter/Spirit of Truth like the world knows nothing about. See Note 73 "Divine Presence".
7. Divine healing. Now this has a mysterious reputation, maybe even controversial. But I have experienced it & know for sure that God heals whenever & whoever He wants to. Jesus healed lots of folks before he went to the cross. He is still in the same business. "Jesus Christ is the

same yesterday and today and forever." (Hebrews 13:8). See Note 132 "Divine Healing".
8. The Church. This is a real big benefit for Christians. It offers worship services, fellowship, much teaching about Divine issues, a place for baptisms, weddings, funerals, outreach to the poor, and professional counseling, among other things. Then it has a built-in moral code for the family, (which is very valuable). Any community is lucky to have churches regardless of the denomination. See Note 49 "Which Church Is Right?"
9. Peace. This is something money can't buy. It is a gift from above & the scriptures say a lot about it, Old & New Testaments. See Isaiah 26:3, John 14:27, Romans 15:13 just to begin the subject of peace.
10. Eternal life in Heaven. Money can't buy this one either. Jesus talked a lot about heaven so if there is no heaven then Christ is a liar. But that's not possible. Jesus was & is TRUTH incarnate. And Heaven is a prepared place for prepared people. See Note 12 "Seven Wonders of Heaven." For a picture of it see Revelation 21 & 22.

To conclude & summarize the 10 benefits above one can say that the Blessing of God is in it for me. And that ain't bad anyway you look at it. Whether the blessing is coming at us from points 1-10 or radiating down from another dimension, ABOVE. I believe it's both & I like it. You will too. Choose Jesus - He is Alive. (Rev 3:20) "Behold, I stand at the door & knock; if any one hears my voice and opens the door, I will come in to him and eat with him, and he with me. (Psalm 68:19 KJV) "Blessed be the Lord, who daily loadeth us with benefits . . ." Also Psalm 103 clearly says "What's In It For Me?"

29
NATION OF CANNIBALS *

In the jungles of Africa and South America and elsewhere cannibalism has occurred for thousands of years. Some recent studies show that even in the U.S. some Native American tribes have practiced this dark habit. But in the present day U.S. where we are educated (we think) and advanced enough to be world leaders and have an international space station orbiting the planet, do we dine on each other?

Well how about Wall Street executives raiding pension funds for hundreds of millions of dollars for their extravagant bonuses? D.C. Politicians lying for votes then doing anything in office? Gridlock up there because the parties are determined to be anything but bi-partisan. (Our system was designed for compromise.) A court system not concerned as much with truth & justice as with personal power, and job security for very expensive lawyers & judges & jail systems, (which are jam packed – my cousin recently got 34 years for an offense reason called for maybe 5 years.) How about our professional gossip system media which focuses mainly on sensational and or liberal stories, and jumps on issues that scandalize (and eats) the church. Then we have a medical system that is so expensive that it practically owns (and eats) all of us. The massive wave of greed (which causes inflation), in ALL sectors the last 6 or 8 years says only negative things of our human nature. "And what shall I more say? for the time would fail me to tell of" - family feuding, domestic abuse, unfriendly neighborhoods, scam artists, dope pushers & pimping, a predacious alcohol industry, predacious credit industry, predacious taxation, road rage incidents, various kinds of sharks, etc., etc... See Note 24 "Who Can You Trust".

Can any nation survive without teamwork and love and mutual respect among its people? I recently heard a Mexican national immigrant say he was leaving this country due to the corruption here . . . When I was a boy some 50 years ago in Phoenix, Arizona there was a scriptural reference on television at the close of the day's broadcast – (Psalm 33:12) "Blessed is the nation whose God is the Lord." They don't seem to broadcast that anymore – it's not politically correct. Neither are Biblical references & plaques in court rooms or on municipal buildings. Have we become a godless "nation of cannibals" where dog eat dog is the right way to live, or are we just a dying country? Either way it's not good . . .

We need a revival of religious values if we hope to survive much longer. The late (great?) Michael Jackson had these lyrics in one of his early songs - "we must bring salvation back." He was right if we expect to turn things around and cause the "cannibalism" to cease. Second Chronicle 7:14 KJV says, "If my people, which are called by my name, shall humble themselves, and pray, and seek my face, and turn from their wicked ways; then will I hear from heaven, and will forgive their sin, and will heal their land." Wise advice some 3 thousand years ago but still valid today. Now any national revival has to start with the individual. Are YOU saved?? If not, why not?? Salvation is free – Jesus has already been offered for your sin and mine. We only need to reach out and take hold of the provisions God has in place for us. (Revelation 3:20) "Behold, I stand at the door and knock, if any one hears my voice and opens the door I will come in to him and eat with him and he with me." (Acts 4:12 KJV) "Neither is there salvation in any other for there is none other name under heaven given among men, whereby we must be saved." See also link #28 "What's In It For Me?" Choose Jesus and his salvation package. Do your part to stop the "cannibalism". Consider involvement in a Bible believing church & support it.

Many other titles: www.gospelnotes.net

* Am I mad, to see what others do not see, or are they mad who are responsible for all that I am seeing? Leo Tolstoy, Russian writer 1828-1910.

30
CHRISTIAN GIVING

One of the first things we run into in church is the subject of giving. And its O.K. for the baskets or offering plates to be passed around - the church organization is a good thing and needs money to run on. No town or city subsidizes the church (EXCEPT the military church facilities and staff.) But in my experience, too often the subject of giving is abused by preachers who intend to "beat the bushes" and cause folks to give more than they might be able to. I've heard them say "put your offering on your credit card and God will help you pay it back." One of the worst statements was this, "we should get a big truck and go to our church member's homes & pick up the appliances & furniture they have bought with God's tithe." (That guy preached strict religion but was not able to live it himself - he was fired for chasing church women.) Another raunchy line is this "you haven't given God one dime until you have paid your tithe."

Well it's a sad day in church when leaders use such tactics but it's all too common. First we need to realize that the Bible is written in two parts- the OLD TESTAMENT and the NEW TESTAMENT. The Old Testament/covenant was stricter on most subjects including giving. The New Testament/covenant reflects the age of grace and is more about God's love & providence for us. While it's O.K. to consider Old Testament teachings on any subject, we should mainly get our doctrine for living from the New Testament. Too many preachers build up a GUILT mentality by focusing on O.T. teaching on giving.

Why not look at what Jesus Christ had to say on the subject: "Give and it will be given to you; good measure, pressed down, shaken together, running over, will be put into your lap. For the measure you give will be the measure you get back." (Luke 6:38) Now He didn't say "pay what you owe or be damned." He said give and you will be blessed. I have personally experienced this system for about 45 years & it works quite well. The Apostle Paul, who wrote much of the New Testament said this "he who sows bountifully will also reap bountifully. Each one must do as he has made up his mind, NOT RELUCTANTLY or UNDER COMPULSION, for God loves a cheerful giver." (2 Corinthians 9:6-7) Those two passages contain the whole teaching and spirit of New Testament giving. Unfortunately they are rarely mentioned in church! This is why it's so important to read the Bible for yourself!

Now I believe God is giving us a choice or a decision to make on the subject of giving. We can give a little or a lot. I think common sense is BIG here. Give a reasonable amount & don't worry about what someone else might be giving or saying. Yes, the Old & New Testaments mention 10% but that is a goal or commitment that can be worked up to as we see God increasing our ability to give. And if we honor God with our resources, He has promised to increase those resources. Here are some other Old & New Testament references on the subject:

- Proverbs 3:9-10 KJV "Honor the Lord with thy substance, and with the first fruits of all thine increase; So shall thy barns be filled with plenty, and thy presses shall burst out with new wine." Solomon, son of David.
- Proverbs 11:4 "Riches do not profit in the day of wrath, but righteousness delivers from death".
- 2 Corinthians 9:11a "You will be enriched in every way for great generosity, . ." Paul, the greatest mind of the New Testament.

The bottom line in Christian giving is coming to grips with God's economics. And it is an amazing subject as any economist will tell you. Just think of the main verse in the New Testament - John 3:16, "God so loved the world that He GAVE his only son, that whoever believes in Him should not perish but have eternal life." Now that was giving in the purest sense of the word. And look at the growth of the Christian movement since that bloody day. Choose Jesus and His principles - they are Alive. See also "Hazards Of Giving" Note 131.

31

ROOTS

Roots are important. Everyone has a family tree & basically have 2 immediate origins – mother & father. Then there are 4 origins – grandparents on mother's side and grandparents on father's side. Plants also have roots that spread out. Generally, the stronger the root the more healthy the plant. If you want to nourish the root there is a product called Miracle Grow for the roots. If you want to kill the plant, get rid of the root – Round Up weed killer. It kills the root.

Then there are abstract kinds of roots. People have orientations, habits, and attitudes that are deep roots. We all have evil ones and good ones. Selfishness, lies, hate, rage, promiscuity, profanity, vengeance, greed, etc. are examples of evil roots. The product – (out growth) of this root is typically a life of striving & straining, pushing moral & ethical limits, cheating, and only being as organized & productive as one has to be to get by. Sometimes, the evil root grows too strong & people push the limits too far which often means jail time. And it appears that jail doesn't usually "cure" people, going by the high rate of return. Some "birds" have been over sentenced & return to society with anger which can & does make the evil root stronger. Benjamin Franklin said, "Anger leads to shame". And the bad root can and does ultimately lead to hell.

On the good side is the root of faith & truth. Love of God & righteousness, the work ethic, family values, forgiving & loving others, and lawfulness are examples. This root appears to produce a more healthy lifestyle of stability, productivity, & progress toward goals. Not only on the individual level, but also at the family level. We can feed our good roots in our thought life. "whatever is true, whatever is honorable, whatever is just, …pure, …lovely, …gracious, if there is any excellence, if there is anything worthy of praise, think about these things." Philippians 4:8 Many of the people on the good side have strong religious values, and the good root can and does ultimately lead to heaven.

Now it would appear helpful for all individuals to periodically examine their roots. We all have an assortment of good & evil roots. The question is, which side is the strongest? Are my good roots stronger or the bad ones? Many folks see a problem or issue on the bad side and make a resolution to change. That makes sense & it's a nice plan but too often we don't have the POWER to control our ROOTS (or the resulting destiny). Resolutions usually last about a week then flop.

God offers us <u>power</u> to nurture the good roots and starve the bad roots. "As many as received him (Jesus), to them <u>he gave power</u> to become the sons of God, even to them that believe on his name." (John 1:12) "Therefore if anyone is in Christ, he is a new creation (Miracle Grow on the roots), the old has passed away, behold the new has come." (2 Corinthians 5:17) "You <u>shall receive power</u> when the Holy Spirit has come upon you; and you shall be my witnesses . . ." (Acts 1:8) We are all making choices from day to day that affect our destiny – this is the very reason we are on this planet. Some will say, "I'm not making choices one way or the other, I just live natural." Well Jesus said, "He that is not with me is against me; and he that gathereth not with me scattereth abroad." (Matthew 12:30 KJV) That means the bad root is being fed. Going back to the first sentence - "Roots are important,"- it only makes sense to nurture the good ones & starve the bad ones, if we care about our future. Why not cultivate the good root so that it supports the plant all the way to the "city in the sky"? (This "ROOTS" analogy is almost on track with the "Jack in the Bean Stock" adventure.) But I don't expect to find giants in heaven – just redeemed people, and the King of course. Choose Jesus he is Alive, and get your roots blessed. See also "House Plants", Note 4.

32

RELIGION DIVIDES

One of the surest facts of life is the title of this page. Catholics distrust Baptists, Methodists distrust Charismatics, Jews distrust Lutherans (and Nazis), Mormons distrust fundamentalists, and Adventists distrust everybody. And it's a sad fact because the vast majority of all religion does far more good than evil. So why is there division? Probably because all religions tend to be very complicated systems of thought and people may not have the capacity or time to understand other slants on the subject. Then a lot of folks just like to argue. Then we have the Bible which can be (and is) analyzed to the nth degree to determine who is wrong & right. But if God is LOVE & MERCY, we too should display those traits in dealing with the subject to avoid division.

I believe one of the main challenges of life is how to disagree gracefully and still be friends (or friendly.) My cousin who is a successful Catholic missionary nun says, "We need to stop fighting each other." We should focus on what we have in common and not all the negative dividing minor points. We should know exactly why & what we believe, but have diplomacy, grace, and avoid ugliness, judgment, and division. (After all, God is the real judge & he might think we fall short too) Romans 3:23.

Now Jesus Christ came along about 2000 years ago for many reasons. One important reason was to create division in religion. See Matthew 10:34. And when He said "I am the way, and the truth, and the life; no one comes to the Father but by me." John 14:6, the "atomic bomb" was dropped. And His statements of deity are exactly why he was executed. But He knew his purpose. "I am the good shepherd, the good shepherd lays down his life for the sheep." John 10:11. He was generous enough to carefully explain his thinking - all four gospels are loaded with his thoughts. He was generous enough to give healings & raise 4 folks from the tomb & coffin. He usually avoided direct controversy by speaking in parables. And he faced rank division with the Pharisees with grace & dignity. But he was uncompromising - even to death for his cause. And he rose from the dead to fully authenticate his mission.

Now too many people in their religious zeal think they are on a martyr mission also. But that attitude does divide. Jesus is the savior - we are not. In view of the peaceful nature of Christianity, we should be peacemakers (Matthew 5:9) and not division makers. I have seen rude arguments and a hateful spirit on the doorstep of the home when religious peddlers come by. I avoid that "like the plague." Ugly division only does more evil than good. And the clergyman with advanced degrees who focuses on why all others are wrong is a pitiful case of divine love & character. Having tact and diplomacy (and avoiding battles) seems to be more useful virtues. Yes, we may have the audacity to hold firmly to that "lost & saved" stuff, and various Bible doctrines, but there is a real need to be discreet & avoid "division." Among other things American poet Walt Whitman (1819-1892) said, "…argue not concerning God."

This essay is not an appeal for ecumenical thought (but I do lean in that direction). It is not to say that all religions alike lead to God. The point is this - when anyone makes a stand with & for Jesus, regardless of denomination, they will quickly learn about religious division, but the worst of it can be avoided. It can be avoided by focusing on the love & divinity of Christ & not the pettiness & politics of religion. Take the high road. Choose Jesus & his Spirit – they are Alive. And just love some of those you are supposed to hate. See also "Love & Hate" Note 124.

33

MY MIRACLES

These events are defined as "something that appears unexplainable by the laws of nature and so are held to be supernatural in origin or an Act of God." Why do miracles happen? Probably to get our attention and change our lifestyle. How does one act or respond when a miracle happens? Various ways for sure, but they do make an impression and stick in the memory.

Since I left home in about '69 there have been a lot of these events in my life. Some of them were religious in nature and associated with prayer, but as often they just happened without notice. (Someone else was praying for me. . .) In '69 two mysterious visions, (one of heaven & one of a demon) may have been my miracle "kick-off." Shortly after that an angel steered my VW when I was too plastered with dope & booze to keep it on the freeway. I could feel someone or something else steering, but I was alone in that car! I prayed for leg &foot healing in Army basic when my arches failed & the 10 mile forced march was nowhere near ended. I felt strength flow into my legs from the knees down (where the bad pain was) & I finished the march & basic without being recycled. I quietly prayed for a crosswind one afternoon when we were in an Army jeep behind a tracked vehicle which was making terrible dust & I couldn't see to drive. That was the boldest miracle - the whole immediate air mass seemed to just lift and shift its direction exactly as I said "amen." Our radiator busted in the middle of the core as we entered Yellowstone Park in our rusty '59 Ford pick-up. We prayed for a solution & God fixed that radiator - it never leaked again till I put in another one 2,000 miles later. Jesus showed me his hands one night with nail holes in the palm. I had been stressed out because the chaplain didn't want me discussing religion while on duty in the chapel. A few years later in a spiritual dream I saw some of the art of heaven. In another spiritual dream I saw my deceased mother playing an organ in heaven (which was one of her hobbies in life.) On a cruise ship I heard an angel speak to me about our adoptive daughter. Recently my right knee was becoming seriously painful & was healed after prayer at church. This list is only some of the miracles we have experienced. We would be glad to discuss any of these if someone wants more details.

Now it is amazing to me that most church people & even clergy seem to be uneasy when the miracle subject is mentioned. Maybe they associate the subject with fanaticism or Pentecostalism or mental delusions. But the Bible has miracles from cover to cover, Old Testament and New. I don't have any problem believing in Biblical accounts of the miraculous - especially since my experience tracks well with Scripture. It may be that some modern minded people & debominations have a faith block (something like a mental block) Mark 6:5-6. Maybe they just don't want to go out on a limb for Jesus. But I will - even if it breaks off. See Job 13:15 KJV.

Have faith in God and the salvation of Jesus Christ. Be open to miracles and let the Spirit "flow" in your life. My faith experience has been an adventure I wouldn't change, critics notwithstanding. See Revelation 3:20, Matthew 18:19, Mark 11:22-24, Hebrews 13:8 The New Testament is LOADED with miracle stories and I figure those people were no different than we are. They had needs - we have needs. God wants to supply our needs and He may choose to use the miraculous. I'll take whatever He supplies because I know He is a good God & will frequently exceed my expectations. He'll exceed yours too. Choose Jesus & His Spirit - they are Alive. Also see Note 7 "I Saw The King."

34

DIABOLIC CHURCHES

In 1966 in San Francisco, California a man named Anton S. LaVey started the First Church of Satan. Since that time, this movement has multiplied considerably until now there are hundreds of such groups of various names. These churches have many of the expected teachings and generally consider their religion a religion of today. Now, many people don't believe in such "silly myths" as Satan, but if he is real it seems likely that some would follow him in such a fashion.

In spite of the "revival" mentioned above, for centuries there has been in nearly all cities and towns, about as many diabolic churches as conventional ones. They compete with conventional churches and in many respects imitate their services. These diabolic churches have well attended fellowship meetings, not as much on Sundays, but all other days – especially evenings. Their members are quite faithful attendees, and often out-do conventional church- goers. These churches have an elaborate music program of loud hymnology which provides much of the doctrine taught. The traditional altar in these churches is much longer than conventional altars. Many of the worshipers sit at these altars. Libations of many varieties are available, and offerings are generally collected when libations are dispensed. By "dancing in the spirit(s)," some of these churches even imitate conventional charismatic groups. Now, the distressing fact of all this "diabolic" worship is that instead of promoting God's blessing as do most conventional churches, these meetings promote Satan's curse on mankind. This of course, is in order since his objective is "to steal, and to kill, and to destroy." (John 10:10a KJV)

The reader should realize by now that the diabolic churches described are bars and night clubs. Of course, this whole concept may seem ridiculous to many, but the connection is especially real in the practical respect. These "churches" promote blasphemy, addictions, loose living, divorces and broken homes, highway slaughter, and full surrender to very real evil spirits (demons) through drunkenness/alcoholism. Many in this crowd deny Satan's existence and power over them, but that makes our adversary no difference at all, as long as he ruins their lives and wins their souls. Consider the words of "Wine is a mocker, strong drink a brawler; and whoever is led astray by it is not wise." (Proverbs 20:1)

Why not avoid those subtle snares of death and plug into the Lord

Jesus Christ and His blessings for time and eternity: The Bible is clear, As many as received him, to them gave He power to become the sons of God, even to them that believe on his name.: (John 1:12 KJV) "He who gives heed to the word will prosper; and happy is he who trusts in the Lord." (Proverbs 16:20) For God so loved the world, that he gave his only begotten Son that whosoever believeth in him should not perish, but have everlasting life." (John 3:16 KJV) Choose Jesus Christ and His churches. There is life there, and hope. And the rest of that John 10:10 ref. above is where Jesus says "I am come that they may have life, and have it more abundantly." See also Note 73 "Divine Presence".

35
FREEDOM IN FORGIVENESS

"Put the anger down and step away from the pain and nobody gets hurt." I imagine an angelic policeman might yell at us through a bullhorn. God directed us to forgive. Not once, not twice, not even seven times. Jesus told Peter to forgive seventy times seven. As a matter of fact, God's forgiveness for us, is in some ways connected to our forgiveness of others (see parable in Matthew 18:23-35). Our response is often "But I already forgave so and so". Our words ring hollow because too often the very thing we forgave keeps rearing its ugly head in our lives long after the offense occurred. <u>With our minds and memory</u> we resurrect the pain and hurt and relive it thereby giving it new life. There by granting permission for the memory to hurt us again. (See "Dragons of the Mind" Note 185.) When we truly release those hurts and frustrations to God we shall not be tormented again. If we give them to God and then some "trigger" comes along to cause that pain to resurface we take it back away from God, and God being a gentleman, He lets us have it back. At that moment we need to give it back to God, forgive again the one who offended us and get on with our lives.

It is our pride and arrogance that makes us wrap ourselves in that mantle of guilt and shame. That sense of "Oh, look at how miserable I am!," the comfort of being a "victim", and all its accompanying pity, draws US back to the old proverbial vomit, like a dog. Cast it away, and when it comes back, cast it away again. Get "Freedom in Forgiveness." The Lord's Prayer directs us to Forgive ". . . forgive us our debts as we forgive our debtors." (Matthew 6:12) Jesus points out both sides of the same coin. We forgive, we are forgiven. By forgiving we grant ourselves Freedom. God loves his children. He does not want US to relive the pain again. Forgive and give it to God. If you need to, forgive again, and again. God forgives US over and over, who are we to do otherwise?

How to do it. <u>There is Power in the spoken word</u>. God spoke the world into existence. Jesus cast out demons with the spoken word. Jesus calmed the storm at his spoken word. With our words we have the power to heal or hurt. With our words we Bless and curse. We shall be held accountable for every word we utter (Matthew 12:36). "The tongue has power of life and death, and those who love it will eat it's fruit." (Proverbs 18:21 NIV). To get healed, speak out loud "I forgive so and so, who has done whatever. I place this act into God's hands and I will trust God to deal with it," or "I forgive this person for the offense that I have allowed to continually hurt me. I ask for Blessing on that person." Or Pray both.

We convince ourselves we deserve to be angry, we think "Wasn't I wronged? Wasn't I hurt? Wasn't I . . .?" And the anger seethes. The anger becomes like rottenness to our bones. "A cheerful heart is good medicine but a crushed spirit dries up the bones." (Proverbs 17:22 NIV) Our self righteousness turns to pride and our pride kills us. "Everyone who is PROUD in heart is an abomination to the Lord." (Proverbs 16:5 KJV)

The Lord of the universe desires your happiness. He has given you the power to be healed. He has given you the power to forgive. <u>If you struggle to forgive, ask God for the strength to forgive</u>. God will appreciate the conversation and you will be blessed with Freedom. Don't delay, your last day on earth could be any day. Live the rest of your life in Freedom - Forgive! Of course knowing Christ makes forgiveness a lot easier -- Choose Jesus, He is Alive.

* * Andrew B. Hellman * *

36

WHAT IS HYPOCRISY?

I was the Assistant for an Army chaplain named John S. & he referred to Christians as "dirt-bags for Jesus." That might have been his way of saying we are capable of hypocrisy. Now John was one of the finest chaplains I ever knew. And he might have been on to something there, even if it is a little derogatory. I have considered his theory for over a decade to make the following reflections.

Lots of folks make a commitment to Christ by sincere adult decision or choice then carelessly fall into thoughts & actions that smear the Lord and his church. HYPOCRISY is no new thing. We slip, some slide, but all of us are less than perfect. I think human character is flawed by nature. This is truly a planet of misfits. And when we get religion the problem is not totally fixed. Too often us "dirt-bags for Jesus" encounter a tough situation or temptation where we should look to God, but instead we look around to see if anyone is watching. . . Well the world is always watching and quick to notice and unforgiving of our sins.

It might be in order to mention that some of the most brilliant humans of all time had issues with hypocrisy or inconsistency: David seducing Bathsheba & having her husband killed, Dr. Jeckle & Mr. Hyde, Liberace & gender issues, Churchill & alcoholism, the professional airline pilot who ran his wife thru a brush chipper, the protestant pastor in Dallas who strangled his wife brain dead then went on preaching, etc. etc. Then on the grand scale we have the mother church disaster sin of all time – the Spanish inquisition. History is replete with cases of human character flaws at all levels. Average Christians are not the only "dirt-bags" around.

Of course God sees everything small or great – we can't hide. He has watched HYPROCRISY for thousands of years (and recorded it). It may be one of his pet peeves – Jesus certainly had problems with the Pharisee's inconsistencies & let them know exactly where he stood on the subject. See John 8:44. He also said "And if your hand or foot causes you to sin, cut it off and throw it from you; it is better for you to enter life maimed or lame than with two hands or two feet to be thrown into the eternal fire." Matthew 18:8 Now, not many of us are going to take a blade and hack away body parts that cause us to sin – no matter how intense our commitment. (If we did, there would be a lot of people missing various body parts, especially men). But we need to be consistent and true to our calling. Giving people reasons to despise us and our Lord defeats the purpose of making a stand for & with Christ. We are being watched & we need to minimize our sin.

- "If you want to talk the talk, be prepared to walk the walk." Anon.
- "The Lord looks down from heaven upon the children of men, to see if there are any that act wisely, ... They have all gone astray . . ." Psalm 14:2-3
- "When you vow a vow to God, do not delay paying it; for he has no pleasure in fools. Pay what you vow. It is better that you should not vow than that you should vow and not pay." Solomon, Ecclesiastes 5:4-5
- "The eyes of the Lord are in every place, keeping watch on the evil and the good." Proverbs 15:3
- "But be doers of the word, and not hearers only, deceiving yourselves." The brother of Christ, James 1:22
- "So because you are lukewarm, and neither cold nor hot, I will spew you out of my mouth." Jesus, Revelation 3:16

To summarize – most people know that God's standards are high & us "dirt-bags" have problems. But it is better to risk being a "dirt-bag for Jesus" than to miss the boat altogether. It will be a weak & hopeless excuse to tell God on judgment day, "but Lord, those who claimed to be righteous really weren't, so I didn't try." Choose Jesus, he is Alive & don't worry about being less than perfect. Nobody gets there on perfection, just Grace & commitment. See also Note 87 "Five C's of Romance"

37

WHAT IS PRAYER?

Some think it's a small thing because we've all heard this as an insult, "you don't even have a prayer..." Some people must think of it as magic when they sit in front of a slot machine and pray for the big win. Some people think it's one of the 5 ways to get through life - <u>talk</u> your way through (salesmen), <u>lie</u> your way through (politician), <u>fight</u> your way through (the knucklehead), <u>work</u> your way through (the industrious), <u>pray</u> your way through (the man or woman of God).

Why pray? I think God wants us to. He knows this is a tough world and that all people will be challenged with needs of all sorts. He wants our needs to be met and communicate with Him. "For the eyes of the Lord are upon the righteous, and his ears are open to their prayer." (1 Peter 3:12a) It makes sense that God has his priorities. It seems that the ones who pray get answered-those who don't pray don't get the "stuff". (If He is looking down on 100 people and 2 or 3 are praying and 97 are just fussing & complaining, who is He going to bless?) "Be careful for nothing; but in everything by prayer and supplication with thanksgiving let your requests be made known unto God." (Philippians 4:6 KJV) "You do not have, because you do not ask. You ask and do not receive, because you ask wrongly, to spend it on your passions." (James 4:2b-3).

It appears that us humans are creatures of habit. We fall into all kinds good & bad; smoking, eating, biting fingernails, sex, work, scratching, boozing, doping, church, TV. Well the list could go on & on... But I believe prayer is a GOOD habit & also that it has the POWER to undermine and/or EAT bad habits. "...though we live in the world we are not carrying on a worldly war, for the weapons of our warfare are not worldly but have divine power to destroy strongholds." (2 Corinthians 10:3-4) "I can do all things through Christ who strengthens me." (Philippians 4:13)

Too many people say they don't have the time to pray. They think it can only be done on the knees. Well yes the knees are good "prayer bones", but actually God hears prayer in any bodily position. If we have connected with J. C., God will hear & answer prayer regardless. <u>The attitude of the heart</u> is more important than the position of the body. Standing, walking, riding bicycle, driving a car, lying in bed, you name it. The habit is cultivated this way - pray any time about ANYTHING. I believe regular prayer in the name of Jesus is the <u>heart & lungs</u> of a working relationship with God. For over 47 years the writer of this has experienced God's faithfulness in answering prayer – a few times almost before the "AMEN" was done.

Naturally there are things that BLOCK answered prayer. Sin for instance. "If I regard iniquity in my heart, the Lord will not hear me," (Psalm 66:18 KJV and others). Another thing that blocks prayer is a lack of salvation, but that is easy to fix. "Behold, I (J. C.) stand at the door & knock; if anyone hears my voice and opens the door, I will come into him and eat with him, and he with me." (Revelation 3:20) Choose Jesus - He is Alive. And pray . . . If He has heard & answered me a thousand times, He'll answer you. We are all equal from His point of VIEW.

38

WHAT IS MARRIAGE? *

Is it a contract between two people of opposite sex? Is it a partnership of those two to go through life as a team? Is it a legal & religious institution; or a paradise of physical pleasure for two people in love? Is it a proposition where "what she feeds me I will swallow, where he leads me I will follow (or- what he feeds me I will swallow, where she leads me I will follow?") Is the American philosophy and psychology of marriage working? If so, why are so many folks avoiding marriage and/or getting divorced?

My wife & I have been married for 38 years this month, July 2011. Neither of us were "hippies" as such but we have followed one of their key ideas – "make love not war." Now as concerned with long term marriage, what does that mean? <u>First</u> the negative: (WAR in the house). It only makes sense that "impurity, sorcery, enmity, strife, jealousy, anger, selfishness, & drunkenness" equals war. If the partnership has a lot of those factors it can't last. <u>Second</u> the positive: (LOVE in the house). It only makes sense that "love, joy, peace, patience, kindness, goodness, faithfulness, gentleness, & self-control" equals a setting for long-term marriage. Those factors make a climate for happiness and goals to be achieved. Such as establishing careers, making & raising babies, building the house/paying off the mortgage, becoming rooted in a community, etc, etc. Basically this generally describes most people's idea of happiness & success.

Is there some magic or secret to having that "love" in the house and at the same time keeping the "war" out? We believe there is. Is it an accident that those 9 factors above – love, joy, peace, etc are a word-for-word quote from the New Testament? Galatians 5:22 says "The fruit of the Spirit is love, joy, peace, patience, kindness, goodness, faithfulness, gentleness, self-control." And those factors are an excellent & natural enhancer of marriage. They also purge out the negative stuff. And that impurity, sorcery, enmity, strife, - list of heart burn is a short quote from Galatians chapter 5:19-21.

It's a sad fact of our modern day & age that the youth culture generally shuns true religion. Hollywood also shuns it. And the U.S. university spirit is also anti-Christianity. Successful marriage is in trouble because young people are programmed to reject Christ and His Spirit. Too many folks are looking for the worldly spirit. (See "The World" Note 27). But God calls us to his salvation; then His Spirit comes to us <u>and</u> into our homes. It's a better deal by far.

As far as the title "What is Marriage?" this short essay is not especially geared to answer that question. But it does offer an answer to "how can we make it work better & longer?" That answer is to be Christian & ask for the Holy Spirit – Luke 11:13. (And don't worry about being labeled charismatic. They don't have a monopoly on the H.S.) Choose Jesus – he is Alive & His Spirit will bless your marriage. See also 1 Corinthians chapter 7 & 13 for marriage info.

* The "What is _____ ?" series were written about '11.

39

WHAT IS SAVED?

Sometime about age 13 or so I recall a revival tent & intense preaching on the "saved" theme coming out of it. We threw rocks at that tent in some kind of youthful protest or entertainment. (That preacher put down his Bible & came out of that tent like an athlete & ran us boys down.) I recall a girl in High School who had a bumper sticker on her car "Jesus Saves". Now she might have been the most un-attractive female in that school and the saved message on her car didn't help her image. It was after high school I learned what the word "saved" meant by divine appointment. On a school maintenance crew I was assigned to work with a retired missionary named D.L. who laid the word on me every day that summer. I got "the whole enchilada" a couple years later, just after returning from Viet Nam.

Now, at least two things are clear to me. 1) Before being saved, I wasn't saved. 2) After being saved my life changed dramatically. Concerning #1, This concept rattles the whole world. Man has the idea that he is quite capable & self sufficient. Don't need no "saved", and don't even want to be "saved". "Jesus saves, Prudential invests, so what," – this attitude is prevalent today & I had my share of it. But the missionary D.L. made it clear from Scripture that God defines us as naturally unsaved. (Acts 4:12) Concerning #2, The next morning my cigarette habit was GONE. I could feel the Holy Spirit "high" and my conscience was working like never before. A profound change (2 Corinthians 5:17) had come from divine quarters, not from any resolution or my own power. But I knew I was a sinner & needed salvation. What about the moral/religious man – do they need "saved".

There was a Roman soldier named "Cornelius, a centurion of the Italian Cohort, a devout man who feared God with all his household, gave alms liberally, and prayed constantly to God". (Acts 10:1-2) But he wasn't "saved", and the apostle Peter was sent to him by an angel (divine appointment?) to hear the GOSPEL message. This is what Peter told Cornelius – "he (Jesus Christ.) commanded us to preach to the people, and to testify that he (Jesus Christ) is the one ordained by God to be judge of the living and the dead . . . everyone who believes in him receives forgiveness of sins through his name." v. 42-43 (All of Acts chapter 10 is interesting, but chapter 16 just knocks my socks off.) Now, if this Cornelius character needed to be saved as righteous as he was, where does the moral person come in?? (After all, it was moral/religious leaders that had the Lord Jesus Christ put to death.)

So what is "saved"? It might be useful to look at (Romans 10:9) "if you confess with your lips that Jesus is Lord and believe in your heart that God raised him from the dead, you will be saved." So – "saved" from what? Living & dying without God, which can be a losing proposition. (Ephesians 2:12) It appears from the New Testament that we all need the GOSPEL message & the salvation that flows from it. Are YOU saved? If not, why not? Yes there is a natural pride/ego barrier that can be hard to cross. But for over 47 years I have tried this "saved" lifestyle & found it to be life changing, real, and worth making a stand for & with Christ. And the "saved" might have a funky image by this world's standards, and there is a persecution issue that Christians have to deal with. But the Spirit and Blessing of God on one's life is like nothing else offered by this world, and of course the prospect of Heaven is just too intense to imagine. Then Christ did talk about Hell . . . Choose Jesus, He is Alive. See also Note 28 "What's In It For Me."

40
WHAT IS HOLINESS?

Is it the condition of a bad guy after a lost gunfight with the police? Is it the proper way to address the Pope? As in, "your holiness, I believe Peter was a fine character." Actually, holiness is a main attribute of the Divine nature. It is entire freedom from moral evil, to the degree of moral perfection. Now man has a problem here because he appears in scripture as a fallen being, by nature unholy & sinful. And of course modern man appears the same way. . . And it appears that this world leads us to live & swim in sin of all sorts so we cannot be holy & blessed by God.

In the Christian church of the last couple hundred years there has been a "Holiness" movement. Starting from early Methodists then spreading to other denominations with the emphasis on perfection of character & conduct, by the power of the Holy Spirit. This movement has moved through time "arm in arm" with charismatic groups and is still a significant part of Christian thought & practice. Its message in a nutshell is; live close to God and experience the power of God.

Way back in time, about 2800 years ago there was an incident recorded in Second book of Chronicles chapter 20 which gives "holiness" it's real boost in Biblical thought. The Israelites were challenged by a "great multitude" of enemy soldiers. (maybe 50 thousand.) Jehoshaphat the king prayed seriously, then the prophet Jahaziel gave the word from God, "Do not be afraid nor dismayed. . . the battle is not yours but God's." (my paraphrase of V. 15b) The king believed and had singers march as head into the battle, "praising the beauty of holiness." V. 21 KJV (Now this is a pure faith picture with great suggestions for the practical value of holiness for living & having the victory over our sin & problems.) Scripture records that the enemy forces destroyed each other in the battle – all of them. Then the Israelites picked up the spoil from the dead soldiers – much valuable stuff, even jewelry. V. 25 (This outrageous miracle not only speaks of the value of holiness, but it also speaks of God's sense of humor & His arrogance in answering prayer.) On the "beauty of holiness" see also Psalm 29:2 and 96:9.

Now in this world there are beautiful things. Childhood, natural wonders, true love, good health, (Army retirement?), are some examples.

But if the Bible defines true religion, and holiness is spoken of as "beautiful", that means something. In the words of a current Biblical scholar, "As we grow in holiness we grow in conformity to the image of Christ, and more & more of the beauty of his character is seen in our lives . . . the more we grow in likeness to Christ, the more we will personally experience the "joy" and "peace" that are part of the fruit of the Holy Spirit." Grudem, Wayne, "Systematic Theology". Pg 758.) See Note 10. We may experience some of the other Holy Spirit gifts too. On that note, I had a spiritual dream, (Joel 2:28) about 1981 while we were involved in a holiness church in Lawton Oklahoma. I saw Jesus walking in that church among the pews. That church had blue upholstery on those pews which confirmed it was the church we were attending. That may have been God's way of endorsing "holiness" and its emphasis on having a godly standard in our Christian character & conduct. A popular reference in the New Testament is (Hebrews 12:14 NKJV) "Pursue peace with all people, and holiness, without which no one will see the Lord." Then (1 Peter 1:16 KJV) "Because it is written, be ye holy for I am holy."

    As I reflect on the presence of God and the victory over problems & sin, the "beauty of holiness" just might be the key. "Put off your old nature . . . and be renewed in the spirit of your minds, and put on the new nature, created after the likeness of God in true righteousness and holiness." (Ephesians 4:22-24) Choose Jesus, he is Alive. (John 1:12) says this, "To all who received him, who believed in his name, he gave power to become children of God." That's Holiness . . .

Many other titles at www.gospelnotes.net

41

WHAT IS THE ANSWER?

In response to this question I have heard some reply – "What is the question?" Many people even think it's fashionable to proudly say they don't have a clue what the purpose of life is. I have even heard college professors say this. Before attempting to answer, let's look at what is NOT the answer.

1. Pride. While we all need some pride/self-esteem, it's obvious that excessive pride is why people & families & cities & nations are burning with hate & violence.
2. Possessions/Pleasure. In a hedonistic society and world we may be laughed at if we talk constraint & discipline. Material things like we all need, but an excessive amount can't be the answer. A Biblical character named Solomon deliberately tried to "over dose" on pleasure (even sexual) and concluded, . . . "All was vanity and a striving after wind." Ecclesiastes 2:1-11
3. Power. Seeking status positions, economic positions, leadership positions, political slots, advanced degrees, or whatever, just for the ego boost or keeping up, cannot be the answer if there is a just God watching.
4. Honor. Webster defines it as; high regard or great respect given. A keen sense of right & wrong, integrity, high rank or position, dignity, distinction, fame, To respect greatly, to worship. Too much of this from & towards oneself amounts to self-worship. It can't be the answer if there is a jealous God watching.

There appears to be a world of people scratching & clawing to get the above 4, but the few who do achieve it, only have it temporarily. We recently visited a museum of death called the Catacombs of Palermo, Sicily. Three thousand people of all classes poor & rich – kings, military leaders, priests, common man, children, all ages & all very dead. All had the same amount of what is not the answer – P.P.P. & H. – exactly NONE.

Millions of people have believed – that faith and devotion to God is the answer. It is this mysterious element that lifts us above, and gives the victory. Catholic or Protestant faiths both alike hold Jesus Christ and His values up as the highest answer. Christ personally said "I am the way, and the truth, and the life. . ." (John 14:6) Also, "to all who received him, who believed in his name, he gave power to become children of God." (John

1:12) And, for over 45 years I have seen that the Christian life has its rewards – some eternal of course, but many in this life. See "What's In It For Me?" Note 28. While in Southern Europe we also visited many FABULOUS old Christian cathedrals. They speak loudly of the majesty of God and HIS Possessions, Pleasure, Power, and Honor. It may be that we do ourselves damage excessively pursuing those things for ourselves when <u>the real purpose of life</u> is clear: "he made from one every nation of men to live on all the face of the earth, having determined allotted periods and the boundaries of their habitation, <u>that they should seek God</u>, in the hope that they might feel after him and find him." (Acts 17:26-27) And all those ancient attendees of those cathedrals are dead & gone but another question is "where did they go?" Those who knew Christ went to the land of glory that He spoke much of – because they knew the ANSWER. To shed some light on the nature & character of that answer, see "The Names of Christ" Note 46. Choose Jesus and His value system, they are Alive.

42

WHAT IS FREEDOM?

Those of us who live outside the fences and razor wire of prison have a tendency to take it for granted. Freedom is almost a holy thing and should be loved and protected. In the Declaration of Independence it says something about "life, liberty and the pursuit of happiness," being high ideals, BUT they can all be lost in this hard world. My friend and cousin Andrew (who wrote Notes 25 & 35) was successful and is from a large family of successful people. Having lost his freedom for a long time, he is now able to give "inside" perspective from prison on the subject.

From a recent letter of his -- "My life here in prison is one of routine. The same events occur from week to week and the routine makes the time go by quickly. My variables are visits and letters so those things are real treats and highlights for me. I get a visit from my brother and sister on March 30, 2013. I am real excited for that. My meals are on a six week rotation and that adds to my routine. I know from day to day, week to week, year to year, just what the food offering is for each meal. I have the menu in my room. In a way it is comforting. What I really like to do is study God's word. Now I finally have enough time to really get into God's word as His word deserves. This is not a casual book. It has many layers of meaning and depth. You have experienced this yourself . . . and God used my present problems to allow me to refocus or more aptly focus the way I should have in the first place on God's word. I now realize that my life is not about building my house or running my kids around from event to event. It isn't about my work, it isn't even about my wife. All of those things have been removed from my life. When the judge cursed me with a loss of freedom he in reality blessed me with the most freedom I could ever have. I now have what I should have had in the first place. I looked in the wrong places for the answers and now I have a much better idea of where to find them. Prison is a place of freedom really. Freedom from debts, freedom from bill payments, house payments, car payments, insurance payments, freedom from home maintenance, freedom from car maintenance, freedom from the hassles of life. I pick my own exercise time, my own nap time, my own study time. I don't have to collect rents from people who don't or won't pay for what they have already received. I don't have to go on vacations; I have a TV that can take me anywhere. I don't have to ride a bus, van, car taxi or train. I am free. It is ironic really. I didn't intend it to be this way but I am *happy with how it is turning out. <u>Freedom is not</u> being able to go where you want when you want. If that was the case then a lot of people are locked into place by the economics. <u>Freedom is</u> of the Spirit and you can't lock that down. Andrew H.*

    Now I have heard that "it's not what happens to you but how you take it, that's important." My cousin's <u>attitude</u> about long term incarceration and <u>perspective</u> on the true meaning of freedom is priceless. Many lose hope, and fall into despair, and have a horrible lack of peace of mind in prison.

    I would hope that my readers can appreciate their freedom AND become <u>truly free</u> in Christ as Andrew has explained above. The sin of this world has the power to ruin folks, as an old preacher once said "Sin is the hardest of all masters – it promises happiness and brings hell, it promises joy & brings judgment . . ." W. Herschel Ford (1910-1971) Jesus said, "If you continue in my word . . . you will know the truth, and the truth will make you free. . . If the Son makes you free, you will be free indeed." (John 8:31b, 32, 36) Millions of folks including myself have learned that a connection with Jesus Christ can be an adventure in FREEDOM, regardless of one's circumstances. God's presence & blessing in one's life can change lemons into lemonade. Choose Jesus. He is Alive. And experience freedom from the power of sin, & victory in Christ. True freedom indeed.

43

THE DEMON

In the fall of '69 I was living in a college dorm in Inglewood, CA. While I was not a "believer" as such, there were some strange things happening. A form of levitation, I saw dramatic personality changes, evil presence, etc. It was that time frame when I had two "visions" – one of heaven, and one of a demon. As I reflect back on those days it is apparent now that a battle was going on for my soul, and God was showing me the two paths. It was clear I had a decision to make.

On one occasion I had reached a pot induced form of meditation when I looked across my dorm room to see a unique humanoid creature sitting on my roommate's bed. It was ALIEN – never imagined such a being. He was blacker than any black. Skin real rough & scaly but not like a reptile – it was just ugly. No horns, no fork, no pointed tail, but beady eyes with a penetrating evil stare. He radiated hate and determination. He didn't move, speak or dance or even blink, but I got the message that he was NOT my friend. I was un-read in scripture but I knew that was a demon – maybe the devil himself. A few years later I came across (Lamentations 4:7-8) -- "Her princes were purer than snow, whiter than milk; their bodies were more ruddy than coral, the beauty of their form was like sapphire. Now their visage is blacker than soot, they are not recognized in the streets; their skin has shriveled upon their bones, it has become as dry as wood." (V.8) is exactly what I saw. And I know that afro type people are offended by this "black" image of our adversary. But it was a different black altogether. I don't associate it racially, I do associate it with angelic/spiritual parameters.

After that incident there were several occasions when I was in that state of half sleep at night – stone sober but pressed on by a power or presence of evil. I always resisted it. Was he trying to possess me? Then there seemed to be attempts on my life – military accident style, etc. Having said "no" to that demon, was he trying to kill me?? It did seem that way.

Now we live in a world of obvious good & evil but people are challenged by the concept of unseen entities such as angels, demons, devil, etc. But this Lucifer character can be seen in the Bible from cover to cover and has only one objective. That is "to steal, kill, and destroy" God's creation. (John 10:10) He nearly got me. Lucifer and his demon buddies are no myth.

- "For we are not contending against flesh and blood, but against the

principalities, against the powers, against the world rulers of this present darkness, against the spiritual hosts of wickedness in the heavenly places." (Ephesians 6:12)
- "Be sober, be watchful. Your adversary the devil prowls around like a roaring lion, seeking someone to devour. Resist him, firm in your faith, knowing that the same experience of suffering is required of your brotherhood throughout the world." (1 Peter 5:8-9)
- "Submit yourselves therefore to God. Resist the devil and he will flee from you." (James 4:7)

After nearly 50 years of knowing where the evil comes from, I can say from experience that we can WIN, and live above it. We all have that decision to make which is the first step. "Behold, I stand at the door and knock; if any one hears my voice and opens the door, I will come in to him and eat with him, and he with me." (Revelation 3:20) I suppose the second step is reading the Bible regularly & church involvement. See "Set Yourself Up" Note 20. Choose Jesus, He is Alive.

44

INVISIBLE GOD

We humans live in a world where we naturally experience reality through our five senses – touch, sight, smell, hearing, taste. Then the word tangible applies – capable of being exactly comprehended, able to be treated as a fact; real; concrete. Now the subject of religion or divine things is experienced in a different way because God seems to be invisible. I think religions are seriously challenged worldwide due to this problem. It may account for the fact why there are thousands of religions in this world and much confusion on the subject. If I were God I would try to simplify matters– maybe I'd hang out in space visible like the moon & reach down with a long stick or finger to remind folks of my standards & plans for their eternal futures.

But is God really invisible? If the Christian Bible is valid (billions of people think it is), then He is not invisible at all. Those who read & believe can see God's actions from the beginning. We can see the creation process of Genesis 1-3, the great flood chapter 7, Abraham, Lot & ANGELS Ch. 18, parting of the Red Sea Exodus Ch. 14, Elisha raising dead 2 Kings 4, fabulous other miracles of the Old Testament including Jonah & the whale. Then in the New Testament we have the incarnation - God becoming a man, the atonement of that God-man, then the resurrection (overwhelming miracles for those who think.) We then go to the release of the Holy Spirit in Acts and the amazing miracles of Peter, Paul & Silas. I have personally engaged with God for over 45 years to experience many miracles. (see "My Miracles" Note 33.) For those who read & believe, the awesome miracles of the Bible <u>scream</u> at us of the nature & character & presence of a wonderful supreme being. Miracles are God's signature. I believe He is not invisible at all, He just expects us to use FAITH to "see" Him. Then nature itself reveals God. For a poetic & timeless picture read Psalm 19:1-4.

Now is God distant? That is exactly what many folks think. "If God exists, how can He worry about little old me? I am just a grain of sand on the sea shore." Well, if the Supreme Being can be concerned with the design and health of a deep water shrimp and/or an amoeba, then He can be VERY concerned about me and all the details of my life. It is His immensity that enables God to care for each one of us. However, humanness & our sin can be a separation. "…all have sinned and come short of the glory of God." (Romans 3:23 KJV) I think that word "short" speaks of the distance from God many people feel. It also speaks of their inability to "see" Him. It is my experience and appeal to others that absorbing Bible truth & reaching to God in FAITH is the way to "see" God. ("Faith" Note 75.) It is not that hard to repent from sin & accept Christ's salvation. (Rev 3:20) says "Behold, I stand at the door & knock. If anyone hears my voice and opens the door I will come in to him and eat with him, and he with me. Why not Choose Jesus, He is Alive. See also "What's In It For Me?" Note 28.

45

FOUR KINDS OF PRIDE

The following essay was written in the spring of 1979, one of my first "Gospelnotes." It would appear that nothing is simple in this world of ours. Even simple pride is not so simple, but there's an old adage that says a lot about it. "There are four kinds of pride: that of Face, Race, Place, and Grace." Now some would say that this summary leaves a lot untold, but it does seem to cover the high points pretty well. Especially when most folks can find their own brand in one of these groups or the other.

Taking a look at the FACE variety, we realize that it's all too common. Not only the good-looking are here though. Some of these souls just <u>think</u> they've "got it." Then considering the RACE variety we see a host of folks indulging in this "cheap thrill." In the PLACE group many find themselves. Now self improvement is respectable, but where is the ground for pride with those who were given everything? Finally we see the pride of GRACE. Even God frowns on this kind – "Let him that thinketh he standeth take heed lest he fall" (Corinthians 10:12 KJV)

Whatever variety our pride may be, we often fail to realize the tragedy of it. In fact, pride is probably the original sin. Lucifer himself, the greatest created being in the beginning, fell into it. He was condemned when he said in his heart, "<u>I will</u> ascend into heaven. . . <u>I will</u> exalt my throne. . . <u>I will</u> sit also upon the mount. . . <u>I will</u> ascend above. . . <u>I will</u> be like the Most High." (Isaiah 14:12-15, See also Note 195 "Why Is There Evil?) At the dawn of our history, in the garden, the human race fell into his <u>nature</u>, <u>rebellion</u>, and <u>condemnation</u>. As one looks into the Book, he sees God's feelings about pride: "Everyone who is proud in heart is an abomination to the Lord. . ." (Proverbs 16:5 KJV) "Behold, his soul which is lifted up is not upright in him. . ." (Habakkuk 2:4 KJV) Whoever exalts himself will be humbled, and whoever humbles himself will be exalted." – Jesus, (Matthew 23:12)

From the divine attitude about pride, it would appear to be one of the strongest soul poisons around. Why not steer away from it into the sparkling fresh waters of Divine Life? Christ himself said, "Whoever drinks of the water that I shall give him shall never thirst; but the water that I shall give him shall become in him a well of water springing up to eternal life." (John 4:14 KJV) In another place we read, ". . .let him who is thirsty come, let him who desires take the water of life without price." (Revelation 22:17)

The salvation of Christ is that water. Let's not allow pride of any variety to drag us into hell. "Humble yourselves before the Lord and he will exalt you." (James 4:10) The natural brother of Christ had that to say. A king had this to say "Now I, Nebuchadnezzar, praise and extol and honor the King of heaven; for all his works are right and his ways are just; and <u>those who walk in pride</u> he is able to abase." (Daniel 4:37)

After reflecting on this simple gospel message for 40 years my conclusion is this. If we wish to harness natural human pride (and ego) the most effective means is the salvation of Christ. Choose Jesus, He is Alive.

46

THE NAMES OF CHRIST

I think it's interesting that people, places & things can have more than one name or title. A horse for example – equine, steed, war horse, mount, courser, charger, hunter, racer, pacer, trotter, ambler, roadster, saddler, stallion, stud, filly. The list goes on & on, and various characteristics of a "thing" can be seen in the name. (I myself have been titled many things – not all complimentary). But this PERSON Jesus Christ has 102 names & titles given in the Bible from cover to cover. It fascinates me to pieces that many of Christ's titles were given thousands of years before he was "officially" born.

The following list is directly from my Scofield reference Bible, even though I am not Calvinist. The Scofield compilers put the list just following Isaiah 7:14 KJV which says, "Therefore the Lord himself shall give you a sign; Behold, a virgin shall conceive, and bear a Son, and shall call his name Immanuel." That is a name which means "God with us." Isaiah was inspired to write that about 800 years B. C.

The last Adam, an Advocate, Alpha and Omega, Amen, Author of eternal salvation, Beginning and the End, Beginning of the creation of God, Blessed and only Potentate, Branch, Bread of God, Bread of Life, Captain of Salvation, little Child, the Christ, my Companion, Cornerstone, Counselor, David, Dayspring, Deliverer, Desire of All Nations, Everlasting Father, Faithful witness, First and the Last, Firstborn, God, Eternal Blessed God, Head over all things, Heir of all things, High Priest, the Most Holy, Holy One, Horn of Salvation, Image of God, Jesus, the Just (One), King of Israel, King of the Jews, King of kings, Lamb of God, the Life, Bread of Life, Light of the World, True Light, Lion of the tribe of Judah, Living stone, Lord, Almighty Lord God, Lord of all, Lord of Glory, Lord of lords, Lord of Righteousness, Maker and Preserver of all things, the Man, the Second Man, Mediator, Messiah, Mighty God, Morning star, Nazarene, our Passover, Priest forever, Prince, Prince of Life, Prince of Peace, Prophet, Propitiation, Redeemer, the Righteous, Root and offspring of David, Ruler, Ruler in Israel, Ruler of the kings of the earth, Savior, Holy Servant, my Servant, Shepherd and Overseer of souls, Shepherd in the land, Great Shepherd of the sheep, the Chief Shepherd, the Good Shepherd, Shiloh, a Son, the Son, my beloved Son, only begotten Son, Son of David, Son of God, Son of Man, Son of the Highest, Star, the Bright and Morning Star,

98

Sun of Righteousness, the Truth, the Vine, the Way, faithful and true Witness, Wonderful, Word, Word of God.

Now without being much of a theologian I can say from common sense that a list of names & titles like the above points to a very special PERSON. It's no wonder that our calendar dates from His birth. And He died for my sin, and then a more dynamic class act – He rose from the dead to prove all his claims. All this just knocks me out. I personally met this Jesus (or His Holy Spirit) on Feb 20, 1972 and five years later I got a glimpse of just Who I'd been dealing with. See Note 7 "I Saw the King". My conclusion is simple. Jesus Christ is all those names & titles show Him to be. He is also the answer to this hard world which we are all living (& dying) in. Choose Jesus, He is Alive & well. In spite of hell. "Acquaint now thyself with him, and be at peace: thereby good shall come unto thee." Job 22:21 KJV.

47

THE HOLY SPIRIT

God is a trinity – three in one – Father, Son & Holy Spirit. All major denominations agree to this. The ages before Christ were mostly the time of the Father. The few years that Jesus Christ walked the earth was the age of Christ. Since then it has been the age of the Holy Spirit. The creeds of the early centuries of the church helped to explain the different roles of each part of the God head, possibly showing the balance that is necessary.

In the early years of the last century there was an "out pouring" of the Holy Spirit – many referred to it as the "Baptism of the H.S.". This was a movement where people in church became "filled" with the H.S. & experienced a new power (Acts 2:4), miracles, healings, speaking in other languages they had not learned, dancing around for joy, etc. etc. This new Pentecost has been hard to swallow for most denominations. Typically, they object because of Ephesians 4:5 "one baptism," and the argument that it is a short cut to spiritual maturity. But this movement does have a better FAITH emphasis than most groups, and it could be the predicted event of the last days as described in Joel 2:28-29. This movement also emphasizes the presence of the H.S. in the individual Christian's daily life.

I must admit the validity of the Holy Spirit (even if some accuse me of being a holy roller), because the man who explained Jesus & Christianity to me in '69 was a retired holiness missionary. I reluctantly, but sincerely accepted Christ a few months later. The power & victory of the H.S. came in Feb of '72, a second touch from above. Even though tongues were not a big part of my experience ("Do all speak with tongues?" Corinthians 12:30), divine healing & miracles were a part of it. See "My Miracles" Note 33. My wife & I still enjoy the presence & fullness of the Holy Spirit.

The famous evangelist Billy Graham wrote his book on the H.S. in '78 which I read carefully at that time. Graham & Calvinists feel they have all the H.S. they need or want and don't care to do any "seeking" or "asking" for the presence or fullness of it. To get "filled" they think one must be perfect & sinless, then completely submitted to God and saturated with faith. (Graham's H. S. Chapter 9). When I am able to jump over the moon I will try for the H.S. fullness B.G.'s way. The whole point of the New Testament is that we need God's power to get there – <u>not our power</u>. (Acts 1:8) "You shall receive power when the Holy Spirit has come upon you." And that has been my experience for over 45 years. There are other spiritual leaders who write books on the H.S. Like Merlin Carothers, "Prison to Praise" 1971; Benny Hinn, "Good Morning Holy Spirit" 1990. Their experience tracks better with mine.

The flowing Holy Spirit can be your experience too. There are lots of references to receiving the fullness of the Holy Spirit. Jeremiah 29:13, John 20:22, Acts 2:33, Luke 11:13 & the entire book of Acts. Speaking in tongues might not happen for all, and I personally don't think it's essential except maybe as evidence. But lots of spiritual folks believe the tongues gift is a devotional habit that cultivates the Spirit like nothing else. The H.S. is capable of identifying & proving Himself in other ways also . . . And when you KNOW you have the Holy Spirit flowing in your life, don't let anyone talk you out of it. They will try. And it's sad because we all need that extra touch from time to time – it's very reassuring to know God can & will do miracles, divine guidance, healing, or anything else He wants to in our space. Sadly lots of folks resist the H.S. and limit their experience. (see Acts 7:51)

Choose Jesus <u>and</u> His Spirit – they are Alive. "The Father is the begetter, the Son is the Begotten, and the Holy Spirit is the one flowing from the Father & the Son." Ask for your full share.

48

A CLASS ACT

What is a "class act"? Most folks think it's a job or performance so well done that it has no equal or competition. When a 10 score is perfect, the class act is a 15 or 20. How about the other extreme "class act" or total fiasco? The fire boat burned and sank. Or a drowned life guard at a L.G. training seminar. (An impeached president for lying under oath?)

My wife & I recently fell in the bad "class act" category. We came into Oahu Hawaii on the cheap, figuring we could find military lodging without prior reservations. (Dumb) After checking all options and dragging our luggage for miles we realized we were "high & dry". A last option of sleeping on the beach was also negative – it's not only unsafe & mostly illegal, but it rains in HI; especially in late September.

Enter the providence of God. It is amazing how prayer changes things. And not just the diligent – pray till you pass out kind. But the bashful – praying quietly in your dizzy & tired mind kind of prayer. That's the kind we did. And God changed our lemon situation into almost divine lemonade. We fell into a private A.F. camp ground we didn't know existed. With a small rented tent on a beach front site complete with restroom/shower facility only 30 steps away and a discount convenience market 100 yards away. Then the Lord provided a 4" foam mattress free of charge. And this beach is said to be one of the top ten "most beautiful" in the world, complete with Aloha birds.

Now I realize that vast quantities of people feel that answered prayer is really just a lucky break. They also feel that the essence of religion is only a good positive attitude. But my experience since '72 is with an active God who gives His presence and favors freely (if we are being genuine in our faith). It seems that a lot of religious folks work hard to cultivate a concept of God that is devoid of power, and loaded with traditions of unbelief. The baggage, complications, and junk of some denominations tend to quench the Spirit. See "Church Vitality" Note 82. My experiment with God from 1972 has been simple – BELIEVE, PRAY, AND EXPECT. Maybe this is why my God is a GOOD "Class Act".

"Be careful for nothing; but in everything by prayer and supplication with thanksgiving let your requests be made known to God" (Philippians 4:6 KJV). "Jesus Christ is the same yesterday, today, and forever" (Hebrews 13:8). "Casting all your care upon him, for he careth for you" (1 Peter 5:7 KJV).

God has been in the business of blessing people since Biblical times. Are you receiving your share of His mercy, grace, kindness, HOLY SPIRIT, wonders, etc? If not, why not? The salvation of Jesus Christ is available free to "whosoever" will ask for it. Choose Jesus. He is Alive. Find out why myself and so many millions KNOW that God is a "Class Act". See also "What's In It For Me" Note 28

49

WHICH CHURCH IS RIGHT?

This is a question that's been around for a long time. Incidentally, it was asked by the founder of the Mormon movement, J. Smith, in about 1830. Another question is – why care? Well I think we should care because this age of our calendar time started in A.D. 32, after the resurrection & assention of Christ, is considered by Christianity to be the "church" age, or the age of the Holy Spirit. God prepared this age by appearing as a man, then teaching, then demonstrating his love for us by dying on the cross for our sin. Ignoring the church in the church age is in my opinion a grievous insult to God. The New Testament clearly bears this out for all who read it and think. So which church is right? There are hundreds of churches who all claim to be the "one & only," and almost have a monopoly on God.

- Mormons claim to be "Latter Day Saints." The rest of us are "gentiles" or outsiders.
- Catholics have the mother church position and the Pope, and lots of ceremonial formalities.
- Baptists are fundamental and "right" about the Bible. They are patriotic too.
- Charismatics have the Holy Ghost and the "power" that brings the victory. Praise the Lord. . .
- Methodists are open-minded and allow more freedom to do one's own thinking.
- Church of Christ has the best name above their door.
- Seventh Day Advents have the "right" day of worship.
- Nazarenes have the second blessing of entire sanctification and a "standard."

This list could go on and on. And considering the conviction and fervor of each persuasion, the title question above is a very good question. So to SIMPLIFY the matter maybe the question should be, Which Church is Right <u>for ME</u>?

I believe answering that question is a simple mathematics formula of time. There are 168 hours in a week. If the average religious person above spends 2 hours a week in church, then 2/168 = 1% of one's time. (99% out of church) <u>The right church for me is the one that promotes my maximum</u>

Godly mindedness during the 99%. The 1% time in church should teach, encourage, & spiritualize us to experience & reflect Godliness in the 99% spent in the real world. If that isn't happening, we should go elsewhere for our spiritual needs. (Of course, there are folks who aren't in church for spiritual reasons and none of this matters.)

There are essential doctrines which should be considered in this church age. These probably define that "Godly mindedness" mentioned above. All groups have their favorite doctrines but there is a core that must be present if one wishes to be considered "Christian." (If we aren't pursuing Christ and His Spirit, then anything goes in religion.) The Bible is capable of speaking for itself:

- Acts 2:38-39 Peter said to them. "Repent, and be baptized every one of you in the name of Jesus Christ for the forgiveness of your sins: and you shall receive the gift of the Holy Spirit. For the promise is to you and to your children and to all that are far off, every one whom the Lord our God calls to him."
- 1 Corinthians 15:3-5 "I delivered to you as of first importance what I also received, that Christ died for our sins in accordance with the scriptures, that he was buried, that he was raised on the third day in accordance with the scriptures,"
- Galatians 2:20 " I have been crucified with Christ; it is no longer I who live, but Christ who lives in me; and the life I now live in the flesh I live by faith in the Son of God, who loved me and gave himself for me."

If the groups we identify with have the essentials, and we are feeling blessed and legitimate during the 99% block of the week, then maybe our church is right and it's a good fit. I personally made a commitment to Christ BEFORE affiliating myself, so I/we have participated in many denominations as we moved around the U.S.. Maybe this is why I/we look seriously at that 99% block of time & its spiritual "fragrance." Anyone can "smell" good in church during that 1% scrap of time.

Let's be asking, Which Church is Right For Me. For some there's no question – they are born & raised_____, and walk firmly in that brand of God's light. Others like myself have had more of a search. I suppose a prayer for guidance would help anyone. But of course the first thing is accepting the risen savior. "Behold I stand at the door and knock; if any one hears my voice and opens the door, I will come in to him and eat with him, and he with me." Revelation 3:20 Choose Jesus, He is Alive. See Note 9 "Serving God."

50

THE EAGLE

It appears that people have been fascinated with birds for thousands of years. At the beginning of the U.S. our early fathers debated which kind of bird should be the symbol of this country. Ben Franklin proposed the turkey, but the eagle was chosen. There is something about the character of the eagle that is majestic and strong and just special.

I find it interesting that God refers to the eagle several times in the Bible, starting with (Exodus 19:4 KJV) "Ye have seen what I did unto the Egyptians, and how I bare you on eagles wings . . ." That phrase, "on eagles wings" does something for me. Then in (Isaiah 40:31 KJV), we read, "they that wait upon the Lord shall renew their strength; they shall mount up with wings as eagles; they shall run and not be weary; and they shall walk and not faint." When God uses the analogy of the eagle my thinking tunes in because those birds are at the top of the "food chain" for their species.

SOME CHARACTERISTICS OF EAGLES –

- Eagles are masters of flight. They have inspired man for thousands of years.
- Eagles soar with little effort. They catch wind currents under their wings and practically rest in flight.
- Eagles fly alone. They mate for life like many birds do, but are usually seen alone in the sky.
- Eagles are patient in search for food. They sit and watch for hours then move at the right moment.
- Eagles have 2 sets of eyes. One for distance, one for shielding dust & rain, etc…
- Eagles are thought to be majestic.
- Eagles nest (live) on higher ground, above the reach of most predators.
- Eagles fly higher than any other bird.

In the Christian sense, there is a clear analogy in being "born up," or "mount up," to being "born again" as Christ mentioned in John Chapter 3. Then soaring with wind under the wings speaks of the Holy Spirit empowering us, not our effort. Lots of folks try to be righteous or religious on their own wits & strength but the wind of the Spirit is a better proposition. Often the Christian is alone whether he/she wants to be or not, but God's presence can be quite real & "up lifting." Christians learn to be patient – "waiting" on God's timing or providence can make all the difference in any situation. Having eyes that see the natural fallen world and also the spiritual parameters is useful. "The eyes of your understanding being enlightened; that ye may know what is the hope of his calling, and what are the riches of the glory of his inheritance in the saints." (Ephesians 1:18 KJV) The majestic part for me is realizing that I am a "Kings-kid." All of Psalm 91 paints a glorious picture.

Some of these reflections were covered by an older preacher named Bob P. at a lake resort just north of Phoenix, AZ Oct. 2012. He did a wonderful job. (And it was his last message because he died a few days later.) For some reason a lot of this "eagle thought" had never "clicked" before, even though I love analogies and have been familiar with his scripture references. But an incident in the year 2000 just knocks me out. I believe an angel spoke to me in that half-asleep state, Joel 2:28; referring to our adopted daughter. A young female voice out of the air said, "little eagle promises to be good, daddy I love you with all my heart." So if she was the "little eagle," that makes me the "daddy eagle." Now I KNOW that God does want Christians to think of themselves as eagles.

Well, there are lots of "birds" out there. Easily one can see sparrows, doves, pigeons, ducks, chickens, turkeys, vultures, etc, etc. But God wants us to be at the top of the heap like eagles. He doesn't want us to run with turkeys, especially when we can have divine "wind" under our "wings." Are YOU an eagle? Accept Christ and His Spirit today. Learn what those "eagle's wings" are all about. (Ephesians 2:4-6 KJV) "But God, who is rich in mercy, for his great love wherewith he loved us, even when we were dead in sins, hath quickened us together with Christ, (by grace ye are saved;) And hath raised us up together, and made us sit together in heavenly places in Christ Jesus:" Choose Jesus, He is Alive. See also Note 28 "What's In It For Me?"

Many other titles: www.gospelnotes.net

51

BEING YOUR OWN BOSS

This essay was originally written in 1979 while we were living in Key West, Florida. Have you ever felt like a slave of the system? At some point in nearly everyone's life, they think of being self-employed. Especially those who follow the day-in and day-out routine of highly organized corporation, factory, or military work. The ability to come to work at a decent hour, work at our true capacity and advance accordingly, live where we are most satisfied, and making everyday business decisions ourselves appeals for sure. Being your own boss – wouldn't it be nice . . .?

It is a tragedy that although many of us meditate on vocational or business freedom, we seldom consider personal freedom. That freedom is the ability to achieve one's greatest degree of happiness and fulfillment in life, "Life, liberty, & the pursuit of Happiness." Now looking at the most reliable source of information on the subject we find that each of us has a profound obstacle to being personally free. In fact, natural man is said to be in bondage to the god of this world. "When you did not know God, you were in bondage to beings that by nature are no gods." (Galatians 4:8) "The god of this world hath blinded the minds of them which believe not." (2 Corinthians 4:4 KJV) Paul the apostle was told by no less than the resurrected Christ to go to the gentiles, "to open their eyes, that they may turn from darkness to light, and from the power of Satan to God." (Acts 26:18) Non – Jews are the "gentiles" Paul was writing about. Even US American "gentiles" who are nearly 2000 years from Paul's time.

The Word of God comes across equally as plain and simple on many other subjects also. However, instead of proving its claims by the evidence and trusting its doctrines, people often attack its credibility & authority. This may seem to be a small matter, but it effectively confirms and strengthens Satan's legal claim on our lives. Playing ourselves into his hands is rather foolish considering that his objective is "to steal, and to kill, and to destroy" (John 10:10 KJV) US. And when I look at all the frustration, brokenness, chaos, and general hopelessness all around, it appears that our adversary is doing his job well indeed.

Being your own boss through personal freedom can begin in your life today. Jesus Christ said, "If the Son makes you free, you will be free indeed." (John 8:36) Another spokesman said, "Now the Lord is the Spirit, and where the Spirit of the Lord is, there is freedom." (2 Corinthians 3:17)

Why not receive Christ right now and break away from the lower powers that are keeping you in bondage and seeking your destruction. "But to all who received him, who believed in his name, he gave power to become children of God." (John 1:12) And that "power" will lead to the BEST VERSION OF OURSELVES, and I believe prosperity (whether we become self-employed or not.) See also Romans 10:9-13. Choose Jesus, and His FREEDOM, they are Alive. See also Note 28 "What's In It For Me?"

52

THE GAME *

People like games. All kinds of games & sports. Americans have athletic games, table games, party games, auto-racing games, video games, TV game shows, casino games, etc. etc. We like games. Do we play evil games too? I think there is one that goes on in families & schools that is so subtle that it often is not recognized.

The game of ostracism – to banish or exclude from a group; shut out, shun, disgrace. (Webster) My father (now deceased) was the oldest of 5 siblings. Having the misfortune of suffering 2 brain injuries as a boy set him up for this – especially with 4 younger sisters... It made him mean in attitude. My mother (deceased) also had a handicap as a young girl. She said "kids can be so cruel". It appears that there is a group psychology or consciousness that enjoys this "game": – "We are and you are not..."

This fun human game seems to rise up in the school arena early – 2nd or 3rd grade? My wife refers to the game - "let's be mean to Suzie today." Then in high school this becomes the "in crowd" and the "out crowd game." But it is not as innocent because it forms a more permanent grouping. We have a national suicide problem today as this game can & does lead to bullying which some sensitive kids – male & female, can't handle. One recent case backfired on the H.S. girls when the unfortunate victim of their plot was smarter than expected and took her situation VIRAL on the internet. Ref. Michigan – 2012 "Bullied teen now home-coming queen." Their victim became the home-coming queen with police protection, local & national news coverage, etc.

Now the psychological power–play of groups; and finding the pecking order is quite natural & normal. Secular groups of all sizes need to have a power structure/leader orientation. Finding a person to ostracize may be only a twisted & entertaining form of our natural tendency to seek leadership. Instead of "who's the boss around here," this game says "who's the loser, let's have some fun." But how about the religious family or church group? With a faith commitment and talk about the power of prayer, the goodness of God, etc., do we play the ostracism game?? Unfortunately it will be found here too. I personally believe it is a subtle tool of our spiritual adversary the devil (John 10:10) to undermine and weaken our group. When we should be praying (if we believe in it) for that "odd man out" or "wild card", instead we are often making them out to be the enemy. (Here's a church growth secret for all preachers & denominations – habitually pray for and just love the underdog "sinners" you have, instead of rejecting and ostracizing them.) See "The Underdog" Note 26.

So how can a subject like this lead to a Christian appeal to faith? It can't directly, but indirectly it can. "Gospelnotes" are an approach to evangelism that hopes to use catchy titles, analogy, figures of speech and EXPOSURE OF COMMON PROBLEMS or objections to faith in Christ. The ostracism or in crowd game <u>in the church</u> is fair "game" for me. Especially since so many people are sensitive to this kind of "stuff," and VERY turned off by it. SHAME on anyone who plays these games, ESPECIALLY in the church or a religious family. And I do believe God has a special place in his heart for the UNDERDOG. "He giveth power to the faint; and to them that have no might he increaseth strength." (Isaiah 40:29 KJV) "I know the plans I have for you, says the Lord, plans for welfare and not for evil, to give you a future and a hope. Then you will come and pray to me, and I will hear you" (Jeremiah 29:11-12)

Choose Jesus and his Spirit, they are Alive. Be aware of petty human games and avoid them. "Take no part in the unfruitful works of darkness, but instead expose them." (Ephesians 5:11)

* Am I mad, to see what others do not see, or are they mad who are responsible for all that I am seeing? Leo Tolstoy (1828-1910) Russian writer

53

SAYING NO TO GOD

Thomas Edison said, "I have never seen the slightest scientific proof of the religious theories of heaven and hell, of future life for individuals, or of a personal God... Religion is all bunk." (Quoted in Matthew Josephson, Edison, A Biography) We recently met a modern day atheist named Dan (assumed name) in the Jacuzzi at a lake Resort near Phx, AZ. Dan was the son of a Nazarene minister, and had a sister who was a missionary in Sudan, Africa. Dan was offended to discuss anything even close to religious or Christian subjects. He was adamant in attitude & unfriendly saying "How can you believe anything you can't prove?" Not much later he admitted bailing from the faith after 15 years because he wanted to have more "fun." (Dan appeared to be about mid 50's and poor with an obvious alcohol monkey on his back.) He was classically "saying no to God." Another Edison era atheist named Jack London, an American writer in 1916 and before said "Knowing no God, I have made of man my worship." Jack died of suicide. 1916

Now I recall another character, this one named Dick Lytle (now deceased) who was a retired missionary from Africa. It was the summer of '69 on a work crew. Dick was classically saying "yes" to God. I was not a believer as such – probably headed for the lifestyle of "Dan" the atheist. But at that time I saw something genuine in this old missionary. He was willing and able to discuss religious questions – even my abrasive and disrespectful ones. Dick had rational and friendly answers. He was a man of faith, and had lots of reasons to believe. He also had the victory over this world & life, and no apparent "monkeys". He wasn't rich but he wasn't poor either. He was just a gentleman and possibly a Bible scholar. Dick stressed the fact that we can KNOW, and not just believe. A reference he made was (1 John 5:13) "I write this to you ... that you may <u>know</u> that you have eternal life." And I do appreciate the ASSURANCE we can have in our Christian faith.

When I reflect on the two basic patterns of life – the atheist who says "no" to God, and the believer who says "yes" to God, I would rather be in the "yes" crowd. Here's why:
1. Even though God is invisible, along with future rewards & punishment, He hasn't left us in stupid darkness regarding unseen things. The Bible is <u>loaded</u> with information and encouragement. It just requires faith &

believing to activate the good stuff. See "What's In It For Me" Note 28
2. Even though faith & believing are ridiculed by un-churched folks (and most young Democrats), that kind of response has been predicted by Christ himself 2000 years ago. see Matthew chapter 5
3. Even though believers have to deal with this tough world and possibly a majority who "blow off" Christ & his value system, our Lord hasn't left us alone. We have the Holy Spirit who is the "Counselor," or Divine presence. See John 14:23, 26 and Note 73.
4. Even though believers are challenged by God to repent from & minimize sin, God gives a kind of joy, peace & HOPE that is better than sinful pleasures. (Most sincere believers will agree to this, but of course the shallows & hypocrites will mock.)

I believe a big problem with "saying no to God" is the continuation of Divine displeasure/curse from Above, <u>from one's roots</u>. We all have rascals in our linage & THEIR sins <u>also</u> may count against us (Exodus 34:6-7). But the salvation & blood of Jesus "cleans the slate." ". . . brighter & brighter until full day." (Proverbs 4:18) Finally to conclude – is "saying no to God" (atheism) a rational way to deal with ultimate questions of life? Or is it just a fashionable way to avoid the issue of God, and accountability to one's Creator? God himself may vote with the second answer. "The fool hath said in his heart, there is no God." (Psalm 14:1 KJV) Why not join the millions and millions who have and are saying "yes" to God. Choose Jesus & His Spirit – they are Alive. "Be still, and <u>know</u> that I am God: I will be exalted among the heathen, I will be exalted in the earth." (Psalm 46:10 KJV)

54
INVISIBLE WICKEDNESS

In a scientifically oriented world it appears that invisible concepts are often ignored or given second class status. Recent philosophers seemed to target invisible concepts especially as second class thinking or foolishness. And God is well known to be invisible along with his challenger Lucifer or the devil. T. Edison said "I have never seen the slightest scientific proof of heaven and hell, of future life . . . or of a personal God." (Edison, A Biography) Well yesterday, 14 December 2012, the world got to see some evidence of "invisible wickedness" in a man at work openly. A 20 year old in New Town, Connecticut killed his mother then went into a grade school assault style, and murdered 20 LITTLE children and 6 school teachers, then himself. This incident has to be the epitome of evil.

Of course, this was not the first. The Columbine, Colorado middle school event in '99 seemed to be about the start of this horrible series of mass murder incidents in the U.S. And we are not alone in the world with these events. Western demon-possessed servants of Satan generally use guns. The radical Muslim style is to use personal explosives or (a jet full of fuel) in a populated area & say "Allah Akbar" – (God is Great) just before detonation. I can positively say God has absolutely no part in ANY of those murderous actions. They are the handiwork of His adversary Lucifer or Satan <u>who is invisible</u>. On a positive note – when children die, I want to believe God takes them directly to Heaven to grow up there. Unfortunately, when perpetrators of these events die, their demons go on living to promote evil through someone else.

Why is man so determined not to believe in the invisible? Why do people look at these evil events and not see an invisible mind or design behind them? Why do the current professional thinkers analyze these evil manifestations, and rarely include the possibility that "an enemy (of God) has done this." (Matthew 13:24-28) I suspect the answer is intellectually toxic and has 2 parts: 1) To admit an invisible devil is real, is to admit that God is real. 2) To admit God is real, accountability and commitment is called for. See also "What's in the Air?" Note 110.

We live in a late hour of this world's history. The second coming of Christ is quite close. Devilish activity worldwide seems to be increasing. And the atheistic trends from those philosophers like Comte, Voltaire, Darwin, Diderot, Edison, Freud, Hemmingway, Sartre and others have created a modern day college mindset that God is just imaginary. Well, I believe the scripture that says; "Beware lest any man spoil you thru philosophy and vain deceit, after the traditions of this world..." (Colossians 2:8 KJV) When I was about 18 BEFORE being influenced by the above atheists and philos., God revealed sobering stuff to me personally about the devil. See "The Demon" Note 43. A couple years later He poured out on me Christ's salvation and Spirit. For about 40 years I have been able to see the designs of evil AND good in this world. And God's invisible nature doesn't stop me from believing and being blessed in FAITH. See "Invisible God" Note 44.

The Bible is the source book for spiritual perspective. (Which is why our adversary's spokesmen above, wanted to bury it.) From scripture teaching our adversary is exposed: "He was a murderer from the beginning..." (John 8:44) "The thief cometh not, but for to steal, and to kill, and to destroy..." (John 10:10 KJV) "We wrestle not against flesh and blood, but against principalities, against powers, against the rulers of the darkness of this world, against spiritual wickedness in high places." (Ephesians 6:12 KJV) Considering the spiritual environment, - it is not surprising when some misguided souls cultivate false religion, atheism, dope, evil presence, anger, hate, rejection, arsenals, etc. then become demon possessed, and occasionally do horrible deeds. See also "Demon Possession" Note 168.

So, what can the individual do at a time like this? Simple – starting with no. 1, which is yourself, "...Resist the devil and he will flee from you. Draw near to God and He will draw near to you." (James 4:7-8) If we are open to God's invisible dimension and have FAITH, He will give us answers, renewal and hope. Why let the herd of atheistic thinkers and evil events be confusing. Choose Jesus, He is Alive – and be blessed. Consider joining a local Bible honoring church, and support it. It may also be in order to help promote a ban on assault style weapons. Only the police and military should have them.

55

ABOUT PAYING TAXES

This was one of my first "Gospel-notes," written in Key West, Florida 40 years ago in '79. Since we are still paying taxes in the U.S. (now more than ever), it still seems relevant... Recently, most of us went through our solemn assembly of figures called Income Taxes. After putting off the headache as long as possible, we broke down and took care of the matter. Some made out nicely and got some bucks back, while others lost a few more to their dismay. Oh, the income tax season – what a joy it is.

But there is a man who got his forms like everyone else this year, and used a different strategy. While owing money to the IRS, he attached a statement to the <u>blank</u> forms and sent them in with a smile. The statement indicated that he appreciated the government and believed in paying taxes, and had always felt that way. Our friend has always been a good citizen and hopes it will make a difference to the Feds. We would all say to him, "good luck fella and good bye."

Now obviously, his kind of logic is folly, but the fact is, many of us are like him. You see, in a very real sense God is a governor and He requires certain things of us. Many respond to their accountability to Him by saying, "I've always believed in God," or some similar line. They ignore Christ's sacrifice, ignore Christian fellowship, never give a nickel, and generally live as if there is no such thing as judgment day. Thousands of years ago people were doing about the same things which brought this response from the prophet Malachi: "You say, 'How have we despised thy name?' By offering polluted food upon my altar. And you say, 'How have we polluted it?' By thinking that the LORD's table may be despised. When you offer blind animals in sacrifice, is that no evil? And when you offer those that are lame or sick, is that no evil? Present that to your governor: will he be pleased with you or show you favor?" (Malachi 1:7-9) In another place we read, "What does it profit my brethren, if a man says he has faith but has not works? Can his faith save him? . . . So, faith by itself, if it has no works, is dead." (James 2:14 & 17) In other words, lip service is no service.

Hardly anyone assumes that the IRS is gullible or ignorant. Why assume that God is? "He who planted the ear, does he not hear? He who formed the eye, does he not see?" (Psalm 94:9) It might be added that He who formed the brain, does he not think? So let's give God His place in our lives and see if He doesn't reveal himself to us and bless us. Jesus Christ said this, "He who has my commandments and keeps them, he it is who loves me; and he who loves me will be loved by my Father, and I will love him and manifest myself to him." (John 14:21) If we expect Him to deal with us favorably, we need to deal with Him that way. Let's "pay our taxes" by responding to Jesus Christ and getting involved in a church that honors Him. Scriptures referred to are RSV.

Over 200 other titles: www.gospelnotes.net

56

NEW AGE

This essay was written about '93 while we were living in Sedona, Arizona; the New Age capital of the Southwest. One of the best features of the New Age movement may be the name. People have always liked new things. This religious philosophy appeals to educated and other folks, young and old. It has a modern liberal church "God is Love" emphasis. Then it brings in elements of many major religions, and Native American traditions can be a big part.

Well what's wrong with the Bible? True, the liberal theologians of this 20th century have dismissed much of its doctrines and miracles, and it's surely not fashionable to believe it, but any honest study of religion should logically include the Bible of history. (Go into a New Age bookstore and ask for a copy and see what response you get.) The New Age consistently looks for spiritual truth and light elsewhere, to the nearly complete rejection of the Bible. Why is that? See Isaiah 8:20.

What's wrong with historic Christianity? Maybe there is a lot of confusion when one looks at the "Belfast boogie" - Protestants and Catholics blowing each other up, or the 500? or so U.S. denominations. Maybe the religious complexity just comes with the territory of a modern world such as ours. At any rate, the OLD standard religion is well expressed by the historic Apostolic & Nicene Creeds. Why does the New Age deny them line by line? Who is behind that?

What's wrong with Christ? He inspired Christmas, Easter, and even our calendar dates from His birth. He claimed to be God. He rose from the dead. Logically, the record of His life and teachings should be intensely valuable to anyone considering ANY religion. The New Age ranks Jesus with Buddha, Mohammed, Confucius, and others who have rotted in their tombs. They also usually stiffen when the name of Jesus is mentioned. Why is that? "I am afraid that as the serpent deceived Eve by his cunning, your thoughts will be led astray from a sincere and pure devotion to Christ." (II Corinthians 11:3)

Here's a couple references that seem to apply to the New Age. "A man or woman who is a medium or a spiritist shall surely be put to death. They shall be stoned..." Leviticus 20:27 NAS. (That doesn't mean they are moving to Colorado.) "Those who divide the heavens, who gaze at the stars, who at the new moons predict what shall befall you. Behold, they are like stubble, the fire consumes them: they cannot deliver themselves from the power of the flame." (Isaiah 47:13-14) "Now the Spirit expressly says that in later times some will depart from the faith by giving heed to deceitful spirits and <u>doctrines of demons</u>, through the pretensions of liars whose consciences are seared." (1Timothy 4:1-2)

My conclusion is this: Many people want to avoid the human sin problem, and have spirituality on their own terms, <u>without</u> the reproach of Biblical Christianity. New Age fills the bill. But according to the Word of God, it's counterfeit and has no power to redeem man's unregenerate soul! There is only one way. "Jesus said, **I am the way, and the truth, and the life. No one comes to the Father but by me.**" (John 14:6) Now either that's true or 1) He was a liar, 2) language has no meaning. Neither 1 or 2 are possible. Since life is a schooling and/or separating process for eternity, when we go for religion that is not legitimate when compared with the OLD standard, maybe we are demonstrating to God what He needs to know. Life is intended to be a Divine challenge. And of course, none of this would make any difference anyway if there was no Hell to shun or Heaven to gain. An old divine once said, "No road to perdition has ever been more thronged than that of false doctrine. Error is a shield over the conscience, and a bandage over the eyes." ("Commentary on the Epistle to the Romans", Charles Hodge; Wm. B. Eerdman Publishing, Grand Rapids, MI) Choose Jesus, He is Alive. See also Note 97 "Was Jesus God?" For an in-depth analysis of New Age and it's spiritual darkness see, "To Hell and Back", Thomas Nelson 1993. Research & perspective from a career cardiologist, Maurice Rawlings M.D.. Available thru Amazon.com

57

IMPOSTERS

This world has always had people who "deceive under an assumed identity, or pretend to be other than what they are for personal gain." (Webster) Such as celebrity fakes, the quack or medical fake, political fakes, scam artists, some even impersonating the military or police. And in this modern day we have all seen false church leaders.

We met a church leader in Colorado Springs in '75 who was like a flame thrower behind the pulpit. EXTREMELY loud, hysterical, fundamental, hard core preaching. One comment I recall, "If my daughters get out of line I will ram my fist down their throats, and they know it. . ." He was fully credentialed and on the payroll as an IFB minister. That guy was such a classic that students from the local Nazarene preacher school nearby frequently attended his meetings to see such a "rare" example of homiletics.

I reflect on a character we met in '77 who was VERY intelligent and congenial. He had two masters degrees and was a fully credentialed clergyman in the UMC. Having worked with him for quite a while, I became aware that he didn't believe any of the main doctrines of the Bible. He had very liberal views on the origin & authority of the scriptures, other ways to salvation, Jesus not deity, existence of demons humorous, no hell, etc. The clergyman should be on a MISSION to promote core Bible truths. NOT liberal minded rubbishimo, devoid of saving power.

Then in about '82 we met the classic (false) charismatic. He seemed to be genuine, dedicated, hard working, self sacrificing – that type of minister. The weekly bulletin displayed on the back ALL the conservative Christian beliefs of the PCG. This guy could pray with total confidence & conviction and in the "power of the Spirit." He had me fooled 100% as to his true character . . . He was the worst hypocrite I've ever met. And how about the foul rash of minister/priest child abuse cases – those guys are "imposters" of the lowest order . See Matthew 7:15-16.

An old dead clergyman named J.C. Ryle (1816-1900) of the last century had this to say . . . "Of all men none is so culpably wicked as an unconverted minister, and none will be judged so severely. . . We shall discover by experience that all is not gold that glitters, and all are not true Christians who make a loud profession of Christianity." At any rate it is clear to me now that the false church leader gains power over people and is capable of taking them "to the cleaners." What is the nature of their "personal gain?" The basic 4 things – possessions, pleasure, POWER, and honor (see "What is the Answer" Note 41) I believe deeply that demons who lead people into common sin such as hatred, lying, blasphemy, drunkenness, physical evils, etc., are not the most capable demons out there. The mark of high demonic ability or rank is DECEPTION & DESGUISE to the degree that EVEN mature and intelligent religious people cannot detect the error. Our adversary desires to have "imposters" in places of influence in the church AND Bible colleges.

    The Scriptures are certainly not silent on the subject of imposters. There are examples in the Old Testament and the New. The Pharisees appeared to be generally false. Then Judas the betrayer of Jesus proved to be quite false. The apostle Paul dealt with some real losers in the first century church. But we have excellent guidelines for the church leader in (1 Timothy 3). "Now a bishop must be above reproach, the husband of one wife, temperate, sensible, dignified, hospitable, an apt teacher, no drunkard, not violent but gentle, not quarrelsome, and no lover of money." (v.2-3) People should carefully compare their church leader with that standard and ask <u>serious</u> questions if they have doubts as to his character. And there is a time to break the "tie that binds," (as the followers of Jim Jones, David Koresh & Marshall Applewhite realized too late.) "Prove all things, hold fast that which is good." (1 Thessalonians 5:21 KJV) I have personally been labeled "divisive" by certain ministers. But if they had seen some of the <u>absolute</u> falseness and hypocrisy that I have seen up close, they might agree to my cautions.

    Finally, I would say be Christian & involved in the church. (There are wonderful benefits involved. (See "What's in it For Me" Note 28) But be aware of "imposters" in the church. Too many people have been burned and are turned off to God & His blessings because of rank hypocrites. Choose Jesus & His Spirit – they are Alive.

58
FAMOUS LAST WORDS

The following are the last known words spoken by famous people.
- Beecher, Henry Ward (1813-1887) "Now comes the mystery." [1]
- Costello, Lou (1906-1959) "That was the best ice-cream soda I ever tasted." (And the last.) [2]
- Crosby, Bing (1903-1977) "That was a great game of golf, fellers." [3]
- Jackson, 'Stonewall' (1824-1863) "Let us pass over the river and rest under the shade of the trees." (He had been inadvertently shot by his own men.)[4]
- Malcom X (1925-1965) "Cool it, brothers . . ." (His last words before being assassinated.)[5]
- Marx, Karl (1818-1883) "Go on, get out. Last words are for fools who haven't said enough."[6]
- Presley, Elvis (1935-1977) "I hope I haven't bored you." (Concluding what would be his last press conference.) [7]
- Sanders, George (1906-1972) "Dear World, I am leaving you because I am bored. I am leaving you with your worries. Good luck." (His suicide note.) not Col. Sanders – KFC [8]
- Thomas, Dylan 1914-1953) 'I have just had eighteen whiskeys in a row. I do believe that is a record." -- Welsh poet. [9]
- Voltaire (1694-1778) "This is no time to make new enemies." (When asked on his deathbed to forswear Satan.) [10]
- Mary the mother of Christ: "Do whatever he tells you." (John Chapter 2:5 when Jesus turned approx. 150 gals. of water into the best quality wine at the Cana wedding.)

Now considering that Jesus Christ is probably the most famous person ever born, His mother's <u>last known words</u> are interesting. And if Christ is God in the flesh, shouldn't we ponder those last words, "Do whatever he tells you."? The directives of Christ, first, last and all in between are especially penetrating if indeed He is/was the one the previous list of humans were fixing to meet as their final judge . . .

Here's a few BEFORE the last – "But I say to you, Love your enemies and pray for those who persecute you . . ." "Take my yoke upon you, and learn from me, for I am gentle and lowly in heart, and you will find rest for your souls." (Matthew 5:44, 11:29). . . "If any man would come after me, let him deny himself and take up his cross and follow me." (Mark 8:34) ". . .

Jesus stood up and proclaimed, "If any one thirst, let him come to me and drink . . . Out of his heart shall flow rivers of living water." (John 7:37-38) "It is finished," are the last words of Christ while living. (John 19:30)

The following are the last words of J.C. AFTER His death & resurrection (a one-of-a-kind encore): "I am the Alpha and the Omega . . . who is and who was and who is to come, the Almighty." (Revelation 1:8) "I am he who lives, and was dead, and behold, <u>I am alive</u> forevermore, Amen. And I have the keys of Hades and of Death." (v.18 KJV) "He who has an ear, let him hear what the Spirit says to the churches." (Rev. 2:7) That last phrase was repeated six more times, which indicates the importance of the thought. "As many as I love, I rebuke and chasten. Therefore be zealous and repent." (Rev. 3:19 KJV) "And behold, I am coming quickly, and My reward is with Me, to give to everyone according to his work" . . . "Surely I am coming quickly." (Rev. 22:12 & 20 KJV) The last word.

I realize that the previous paragraphs have way too much scripture refs. for an essay of this length. But the famous person who said that stuff is way too intense not to quote Him excessively. He claimed to be God which is beyond any human's territory. If He really was/is God, ANYTHING He said should be <u>intensely</u> considered, pondered, meditated, reflected, cogitated, contemplated, ruminated, deliberated, head-worked, and studied before it's too late . . . I would love to know what the famous folks listed above would say about Jesus Christ if they could come back and talk to us . . . But they can't come back, & we have to act on "faith" - trusting and acting on the words of that famous person J.C., just as they should have. Choose Jesus, He is Alive. See "I saw the King" Note 7.

* 1 – 10 "Words" from: www.dmsmapping.com/word

59
PATTERNS

There would appear to be patterns all around. Those of industry, business, weather, families, society, governments, military, etc. When my wife & I were in Ephesus Turkey recently we noticed a <u>pattern of EPHESUS</u>. The taxi driver said there were three ancient religions represented within half a mile. The first he showed us was the ruins of the temple of Diana (which was a primitive & sexually corrupt cult as mentioned in Acts 19:23-29.) Only one column remained which had a large bird nest on top of it. Then he showed us the "cold" remains of the 2nd century cathedral of the Apostle John which offered the light of the Gospel at that time. Then he showed us the Muslim mosque facility of the 8th or 9th century which was still in service, but of course devoid of the Gospel of Christ.

I have reflected as to whether there is a general <u>pattern of HISTORY</u> here. In the beginning of time there was limited light from above, and people largely did their own thing. We see the lack of morality/Godliness & the resulting judgments of Noah's ark & flood, then Sodom & Gomorrah, etc. But the light from prophets like Moses & David, then Christ the messiah accumulated. Now for a couple thousand years the Christian "church" has influenced the whole world. But our modern era for the last 100 years or so has shown shocking decline worldwide. And Christ implied in His teaching that the end times (which are either here or near) would show a regression of faith & commitment. "... when the son of man returns will He find (true) faith on earth?" (Luke 18:8) Now we have a host of world religions that have no teaching of Christ, or only a weak residual of those gospel teachings & commitment.

Is there a <u>PERSONAL</u> pattern to be seen in both the above, but just on the small scale of the individual? Natural man (or woman) is born & has limited light from above. But along comes the message/teaching of Christ that being Born Again is possible. (John 3:3) The individual accepts the free offer from above & finds spiritual awakening, truth, personal fulfillment, and blessings from that dimension above. Then with zeal moves upwards on the path of God. (Jeremiah 6:16) But in time there is too often dissipation of that enthusiasm & zeal. Temptation strikes, the adversary blows some lies into his/her ear. "You are missing out on a lot of fun . . ." or "your friends really think you are too religious, and you are pathetic . . ." or "that God stuff is just a bunch of bunk." Serious questioning of one's faith commitment, and apathy sets in. Backsliding into old sinful habits (or new ones) is the typical result. Then we see an individual with little faith, and much apostasy – abandoning of what one believed in.

What I get from the EPHESUS, HISTORICAL, and PERSONAL patterns above is that it is COMMON for humanity to lose its connection with true Gospel faith. This life we find ourselves in is designed by God to challenge & test our character. I have slipped a few times in my 45 plus years of living the Christian lifestyle, and I've seen many completely fail/give up the "good fight." (And according to Hebrews 6:4 it is difficult to recover . . .) But God is very faithful, and very typically finishes the pursuits/endeavors that He starts. If we keep our eyes on Christ and draw on His strength not ours, there will be progress & not failure in the course of time. ". . .to all who received him, he gave power to become children of God." (John 1:12) "I press on toward the goal for the prize of the upward call of God in Christ Jesus." (Philippians 3:14) "Fight the good fight of the faith; take hold of the eternal life to which you were called . . ." (1 Timothy 6:12) " . . . the path of the righteous is like the light of dawn, which shines brighter and brighter until full day." (Proverbs 4:18)

Patterns – they don't have to be discouraging if we are determined to WIN. Choose Jesus, He is Alive. See "Set Yourself Up" Note 20.

60

TRAGEDY OR COMEDY?

When we were living in Key West, Florida in '77 or so, there was a wall plaque in the military day room. "Life is a tragedy to those who think, it is a comedy to those who feel." For many years I have reflected on that philosophical statement. Whether a TRAGEDY or COMEDY will depend on one's viewpoint, and the OUTCOME of the particular situation. Looking at bite-size examples may help answer the question.

- When a woman has a baby (which we did there at that time) there is a lot of pain and medical issues of the worst variety -- tragedy – but then the new baby can be real charming & sweet. Almost a comedy or fun outcome . . .
- Earning two retirements then going to jail for more than TWICE the average time of murder for a crime just a few years ago would have got a couple years in the slammer is a real tragedy. But finding real faith renewal, and spiritual victory is almost a comedy or joyous outcome . . .(just a high price to get that blessing)
- An Asian nation follows false leadership then loses the resulting war by being nuked was/is a tragedy. But that nation becomes prosperous & successful, and not having the burden of funding an expensive military machine is a joyous outcome. . .
- Conservative/productive U.S. Judeo-Christian values giving way to liberal loosie-goosie anything goes policies on every subject, is a real tragedy. The corruption of the U.S. entertainment industry, and pettiness in Washington D.C. politics is surely a comedy (might as well laugh - what other good can we get from it?)
- Handicapped people and the blind go through life with hardships untold which is a real tragedy. But those same people develop character, and often out-perform us "normal" folks - paralyzed pres. Roosevelt of the early 40's comes to mind & is a joyous outcome & example of the handicapped.
- Early Christians were fed to lions in the arena for entertainment of the Romans. A tragedy especially for the victims. But a comedy outcome when the state religion became Christianity and was publicly funded by Roman "acquired" money. Emperor Constantine 1
- The character Joseph long before Christ who was sold into slavery in Egypt by his own brothers had to be a tragedy. But God promoted him

all the way to the second man to the Pharaoh. What a joyous outcome for him & early Israel. Genesis Chapter 37.
- God visits his planet earth in the form of J.C., then gets condemned to death by the religious leaders of that same nation that He started & nurtured with major miracles. The disaster tragedy of the human race of all time. But the resurrection has been a subject of rejoicing for 2 thousand years now. For believers in Christ there can be no better comedy - "the last laugh is the best laugh."

The objective view of life may well be a tragedy with all its hardships, disasters, accidents, WARS, murders, abortions, divorces, alcoholism, (old age), and sad facts with hell as a natural end. It is hard to imagine how that list of muck can be a comedy to anyone (unless they are on a real bizarre drug.) But with the "victory" of Christ's salvation in place, and the under girding of the Holy Spirit, it is indeed possible to feel comedy and fun in this hard world. A lot of unfortunate/difficult things do have a silver lining – especially for those who believe & pray.

- Psalms 94:19 "When the cares of my heart are many, thy consolations cheer my soul."
- 2 Corinthians 1:9 "Why, we felt that we had received the sentence of death; but that was to make us rely not on ourselves but on God who raises the dead; . . ."
- Romans 8:28 "We know that in everything God works for good with those who love him, who are called according to his purpose."
- Romans 8:18 "I consider that the sufferings of this present time are not worth comparing with the glory that is to be revealed to us."

Choose Jesus, He is Alive. And think victory, comedy, optimism, God's providence, blessing, and eternity in heaven. What a fine outcome.

61
OBSESSIONS

I am amazed at some of the extreme hobbies/habits folks can fall into. By definition "obsession" is something like an idea, desire or emotion that haunts the mind to an abnormal degree, and cannot be fixed by reasoning. The strange obsessions below can show something bizarre about human nature.

- Imelda Marcos and her 3000 pairs of shoes.
- Hugh Hefner and his mansion in Chicago packed with young beauties in bathing suits.
- How about the car collector with 50 antique autos kept in perfect condition but rarely driven?
- The lifestyle of keeping pit bulls, Harleys, and assault weapons is among us.
- Some folks hoard tons of junk in their house or scores of animals inside & out.
- How about the "fatal attraction" of keeping lions, tigers, wolves & bears until getting eaten by them?
- Thrill seekers who have to ride the biggest wave, base jump from the highest cliff or bridge, or get in a sleeping bag with the most live rattlesnakes ever (25 of them.) etc., etc.
- A wise preacher would say nothing about the obsession some people have with booze, drugs, & sex. Those things have addictive powers beyond haunting the mind. . .
- Workaholics grinding themselves into the ground working too much.
- F.J.S. sometimes getting up at 3:00 am to write a "hot" G-note title that is preventing peaceful sleep.

Now it is obvious to me that God has an OBSESSION with the human race. He has busted Himself to reveal something of His nature and desires for our well being and eternal futures. And we can see a lot of the Divine nature in the pages of the Bible – how He dealt with the garden problem and the fall of the race (paradise lost.) We see God's <u>frustration</u> with the generation of Noah, and His <u>judgment</u> in washing them all away. His <u>preserving</u> one family to continue the human race. <u>Choosing</u> Abraham to be the start of Israel. Then <u>dealing</u> with the early judges & kings of that young nation. Then His <u>patience</u> with David and Solomon is amazing.

Then <u>continuing</u> David's seed through centuries of national decline & revival to ultimately <u>revealing</u> the messiah or savior. And God inspired writers to <u>record the history</u> of His actions even beyond Christ until the early church was well established – about 300 A.D. Then at the end of the record (Revelation 21-22) we see paradise regained by our race. And I believe that record we call the Bible is quite accurate – see Psalm 12:6

The above paragraph speaks of God's OBSESSION to reach out to humanity, and lift them to higher ground. I admire His nature & patience to allow sinful creatures like us to exist in such numbers, THEN to be obsessed with bringing us to salvation. Man is said to be fallen, and in need of God's touch from above. Maybe it's that "touch" that saves us from ourselves, and unhealthy obsessions.

- "You are not restricted by us (Gospel salvation), but you are restricted in your own affections" 2 Corinthians 6:12
- "Beloved, I beseech you . . . to abstain from the passions of the flesh that wage war against your soul." 1 Peter 2:11
- "God so loved the world that he gave his only Son, that whoever believes in him should not perish but have eternal life." John 3:16
- "Behold I stand at the door and knock; if any one hears my voice and opens the door, I will come in to him and eat with him, and he with me." Revelation 3:20

Choose Jesus, He is Alive. Be blessed, and beware of unhealthy obsessions. Our adversary has "Taylor-Made" bad priorities for nearly everyone. See Peter 5:8

Other interesting titles: www.gospelnotes.net

62

WAXING POLITICAL

Recently we were on the road to Phx. AZ, heading south from the Verde Valley. We entered the freeway between two cattle trucks which were loaded with probably 40 cows each, headed for the slaughter. I found this quite interesting because my mind had been full of confusion over the political re-election (U.S. Nov. 2012). It dawned on me that we were in the midst of cows... Even my daughter voted for him...

It amazes me that people will re-elect a president who has questionable roots, job performance, value system, religious background, wholesale & loose immigration policy, jobless economy, etc... And according to many political analysts, it was only personal charm & charisma that won the election! Then his position on liberal social programs, gay rights, wholesale abortion, legalizing pot, and INCREASING DEBT spending is scary. (It used to be tax & spend – now it's spend, borrow, then tax.) I would say God can't bless much of the liberal agenda – neither can the laws of economics.

<u>Abraham Lincoln</u> and/or William J. H. Boetcker warned of these seven steps to government failure:
- You cannot bring about prosperity by discouraging thrift.
- You cannot help the poor by destroying the rich.
- You cannot lift the wage-earner up by pulling the wage-payer down.
- You cannot keep out of trouble by spending more than your income.
- You cannot further the brotherhood of man by inciting class hatred.
- You cannot establish sound social security on borrowed money.
- You cannot help men permanently by doing for them what they could and should do for themselves.

How uncanny that today's liberal agenda has these exact positions! Someone once said "financial collapse is as good as military defeat." (Anonymous) When I look at the determination up there to spend us into bankruptcy, and a complete smear campaign against anything responsible, I suspect a high – level spiritual conspiracy to destroy this country. The root problem may be a bad spirit blowing over the U.S., and the liberals may be unwittingly serving our adversary. (See 2 Chronicles 18:18-22). This president may have charm and a great smile, but it doesn't fool me. Jesus said "you will know them by their fruits." (Matthew 7:16) There are some Bible students who believe he is the predicted end time character of

Revelation chapter 13. While I haven't gone there yet, I do believe he could be possessed with a high-level demon, or Lucifer himself.

Thomas Jefferson said "The whole of government consists in the art of being honest." There is another agenda when I see the president taking multi-million dollar vacations back-to-back, in the face of a national debt CRISIS. And nowadays it appears that polarization and dog-eat-dog politics is normal. God help us. The Book reveals that ". . . no city or house divided against itself will stand" (Matthew 12:25) Our adversarial form of govt. process was a great experiment for a couple hundred years, but now without the emphasis on God's values & personal integrity, it appears to be falling apart.

Those who care about their country should pray for the leaders to get along & solve national problems like reasonable adults. We should also pray for a leader like Lincoln or Reagan to emerge. We should pray for a national revival – (hopefully it's not too late.) "If my people which are called by my name, shall humble themselves, and pray and seek my face, and turn from their wicked ways, then I will hear from heaven, and will forgive their sin and heal their land." (2 Chronicles 7:14 KJV) And any national recrudescence of religious values has to start <u>with the individual</u>. Are YOU saved? If not, why not? It's just a matter of getting our lame egos out of the way long enough to believe & pray for salvation. The price has already been paid by Jesus when he was offered for your sin and mine. "If you confess with your lips that Jesus is Lord and believe in your heart that God raised him from the dead, you will be saved." (Romans 10:9) "Behold I stand at the door and knock; if any one hears my voice and opens the door, I will come in to him and eat with him, and he with me." (Revelation 3:20) Choose Jesus, He is Alive. And be blessed on the way to glory, even if national politics are on the rocks.

63

OLD AGE

All people deal with the problem of aging in their own way. I suppose a navy man (or woman) might say "my ship is sinking without being torpedoed!" An army man might say "my camp has been invaded by a mysterious enemy that blows toxic dust on my sleeping body – I awake each morning to see more damage..." Actually this problem is not too worry-some in my 62nd year, but it's a sure thing it will get WORSE.

Philosophers have said some interesting things about old age:

- Youth is a blunder; Manhood a struggle; <u>Old Age</u> a regret. Benjamin Disraeli (1804-1881) English novelist
- Age steals away all things, even the mind. Virgil – Roman poet 70-19 B.C.
- Tobacco, coffee, alcohol, hashish, prussic acid, strychnine, are weak dilutions; the surest poison is time. Ralph Emerson (1803-1882) Unitarian minister/atheist
- Old age is the most unexpected of all the things that happen to a man. Leon Trotsky – Russian journalist (assassinated 1940), "Diary in Exile" 1935
- My second fixed idea is the uselessness of men above 60 years of age . . . Sir William Osler, (1849-1919) –British physician (This guy's pen is BRUTAL toward me . . .)
- Time makes more Converts than Reason. Thomas Paine, (1737-1809) - (Tom Paine inspired the Dec. of Independence AND gave our country its name – U.S. of A.)

Does the Bible have anything to say about the "old age" problem? Yes it does. "Remember also your Creator in the days of your youth, <u>before</u> the <u>evil days</u> come, and the years draw nigh, when you will say, 'I have no pleasure in them;' before the sun and the light and the moon and the stars are darkened. . . the strong men are bent, and the grinders (teeth) cease because they are few . . .one rises up at the voice of a bird . . . terrors are in the way;. . . the grasshopper drags itself along and desire fails; because man goes to his eternal home and the mourners go about the streets." Ecclesiastes 12:1-5

My wife & I have been living in retirement communities for over 25 years and have seen our senior friends and neighbors decline and die. My father was with us for a few of his last years. And even though he promoted a senior citizen romance, it just didn't last very long. . . The coming of the grim reaper is a serious & sober fact of life. <u>So what's the point</u>? Well, unless we can find the "fountain of youth" and restore/extend our years endlessly here on this planet, we should all move towards;

- <u>God's answer to life, and old age</u> -

- ✓ <u>According to Paul</u> the apostle, "he made from one every nation of men to live on all the face of the earth, . . .<u>that they should seek God</u>, in the hope that they might feel after him and find him." Acts 17: 26-27 ". . .Though our outer nature is wasting away, our inner nature is being renewed every day. For this slight momentary affliction is preparing for us an eternal weight of glory beyond all comparison," 2 Corinthians 4:16-17
- ✓ <u>According to Christ</u>, "Let not your hearts be troubled; believe in God, believe also in me. In my Father's house are many rooms; if it were not so, would I have told you that I go to prepare a place for you? And when I go and prepare a place for you, I will come again and will take you to myself, that where I am you may be also." Thomas said to him, "Lord, we do not know where you are going; how can we know the way?" Jesus said to him, "I am the way, and the truth, and the life; no one comes to the Father, but by me." John 14:1-6

Someone will ask, "how can that God & Jesus stuff be a panacea for anything, let alone old age?" Well, if the scriptures are a valid revelation of God's mind, then we are placed here <u>deliberately</u> as a test of character. If we pass the test by reaching out to the risen Christ, God will BLESS and ENHANCE all phases of life – <u>even old age</u>. (That's what the blood of Christ, and His Spirit is all about.) And realizing that our decline and demise is NOT the end, is a great comfort. It has been commonly said "Gods people die well." I say they live well, grow old well, die well, then go to a better place to spend eternity. I'm counting on that. Choose Jesus, He is Alive. See also "Fountain Of Youth" Note 108.

64
WHAT ABOUT VENGEANCE?

We lived in a trailer park in Colorado in 1976 with an old cowboy neighbor. Henry (now deceased) told me about a young resident who ran over his dog then backed the car up deliberately over the dog to finish him off. Henry was hurt by this evil action & even at 80 years of age knew how to get even. He hobbled to the culprit's car at 2 AM and rammed a potato up the tail pipe with a broomstick real tight. The next day the young guy's car was mysteriously unable to run. And the next day the wrecking truck hauled it off, never to return. Trailer park diplomacy, poetic justice, or cowboy ingenuity? At any rate, I don't recall Henry claiming to be a Christian or religious.

Vengeance or "getting even" is a serious problem of this world. And in the religious arena it is even more troublesome because God's people are supposed to follow the example & teaching of Christ to "turn the other cheek" (Matthew 5:39). Many proud people avoid Christianity because they don't want to "turn the other cheek." I heard one young believer say "I only have two cheeks . . ." (He didn't stay long in the faith for other reasons also.) And apparently when our guard is down with no means of vengeance, we are more likely to suffer dishonor. <u>Human nature</u> typically wants to know what deeds it can get away with. (See also Note 182 "Human Nature")

Now I am under no illusion as to how difficult this vengeance problem is. Especially as an American, where each man (& woman) is a microcosm of the U.S. with the same attitudes of pride & independence and self defense. (My own daughter was beat-up at school by another H.S. girl, and now is taking oriental martial arts classes.) I am also aware of how old this problem is. We see it in Genesis chapter 4, some six thousand years ago? Cain had killed his brother Abel and God cursed him. Cain was worried that someone would take vengeance against him, but God said in v.15 KJV "not so – I will judge them seven times for that vengeance." (my paraphrase) And there is an interesting case in Genesis 12:10-20 where God DID take vengeance against the king of Egypt because of an incident involving Abraham & Sarah.

How did Jesus Christ himself deal with the vengeance problem? On one occasion He was shunned along with his disciples. (Luke 9:52–55 KJV) The disciples said, "Lord, do you want us to rain fire down . . . and consume them?" Jesus replied, "no – you don't know what manner of spirit ye are of." This event is VERY revealing. Then we have the rejection, torture and crucifixion scenes where Jesus on the cross said "Father, forgive them . . . they know not what they do." his is sobering stuff – especially knowing that Christ is our EXAMPLE. If scripture has meaning, it does appear that <u>God challenges us</u> to forgive/pardon others and let Him repay. "Vengeance is mine, I will repay." (Romans 12:19) -- that thought is repeated other places Old and New Testaments, possibly to reveal the force of it. (I believe I could name at least 7 or 8 dead individuals who were taken out of this life early for their sin against others. But I don't take pleasure in this knowledge, see Psalms 68:21.)

Now <u>if God reveals his presence to us</u> by our seeking Him, then the problems of this Christian value system should not be as thorny – (my experience in a nutshell.) And I suspect God has put issues like "turning the other cheek" in front of EVERY soul as part of <u>the challenge</u> of living Christ-like. On one occasion the apostles had been arrested & beaten for preaching Jesus. They left the council "rejoicing that they were counted worthy to suffer dishonor for the name." (Acts 5:41) That is the true Spirit of Christianity. -- NOT the story of cowboy Henry, or some of my own failures to be Christ-like . .

On a positive note:
- "Any man can seek revenge; it takes a king or prince to grant a pardon." A. J. Rehrat[1]
- "One pardons in the degree that one loves." Francois De La Rochefoucauld; brainyquote.com
- "Good sense makes a man slow to anger, and it is his glory to overlook an offense." Solomon, Proverbs 19:11
- "Though I walk in the midst of trouble, thou dost preserve my life; thou dost stretch out thy hand against the wrath of my enemies; and thy right hand delivers me." Psalm 138:7

Choose Jesus, and His value system, they are alive and offer a better future. For spiritual survival tips see Ephesians chapter six which deals with the armor of God.

---

[1] "Moments of Reflection" by Jean Hawthorn & Mike Walton 1995

65
WHY THE BIBLE?

The Bible is a very interesting book. It is very old, can be mysterious, and is the bestselling book of all time. It is loved and hated more than any other book. It is the final authority for many. AND it is the most understood book in the world without even being read (LOL). "Why the Bible" is a question millions of folks ask. Sometimes it's asked in a negative/critical spirit. Sometimes it's asked in a positive way. Let us look at the negative stuff first.

In the critical mode, people get away from the Bible using arguments like these:

1. The Bible is for ignorant folks especially if they believe it literally.
2. The Bible can't be accurate to the original manuscripts even if they were inspired because no original documents exist. And it has thousands of errors from being re-copied.
3. The Bible is "full of myths" such as 7 day creation, Noah & big flood, Moses & the Red Sea parting, David & Goliath, Jonah & whale, virgin birth of Christ, His resurrection, Heaven & Hell, etc., etc.
4. If I want to be university minded & scientific I must go with the Big Bang theory & C. Darwin. Making a stand for the Bible I commit social/intellectual suicide.
5. How can you believe what you can't prove? (see Note 53 "Saying NO to God")

Now, "Why the Bible?" We should be fair & make a case for the positive too.

1A. Some of the world's best minds were very convinced that the Bible is truly the Word of God. Christopher Columbus, Martin Luther, George Washington, John Q. Adams, Thomas Jefferson, Abraham Lincoln, Woodrow Wilson, John Locke, and thousands of others . . .

2A. For decades I have studied the origin & transmission of the Bible to us through time. One notable book is by a Dr. Neil Lightfoot – "How We Got The Bible." 1986. The objections above are WEAK when one looks at the truth of the matter. The materials used in early writing were mostly leather, vellum, & papyrus, which don't last as long as modern quality paper. Therefore, the scrolls were re-written by scribes & occasionally a slip occurred. But the Jews of ancient ages were EXTREMELY careful in handling their sacred writings. The thousands of errors are <u>because</u> there are thousands of ancient fragments and copies today. People who bash the Bible don't realize that it is the very BEST preserved book from ancient days. (Psalms 12:6 KJV) "The words of the Lord are pure words; as silver tried in a furnace of earth, purified seven times."

3A. I personally don't want to think of those admittedly hard-to-believe stories mentioned above as "myths". Nearly every one of them were alluded to as fact by Jesus Christ himself . . .

4A. The Bible offers HOPE for the seeker of God & truth, (and of course it shows the way to ETERNAL LIFE.) I will take the salvation & Blessing of God any day before the endorsement & approval of the Big Bang/C. Darwin crowd. (Romans 1:18-22)

5A. The last negative argument from above is misleading. The Divine test of life is FAITH, which is a whole different element from scientific proof. To believe is a DECISION we make – NOT a matter of having proof. And God does seem to require faith. But it is given as a gift <u>if we are open to it</u>. See Ephesians 2:8. I can honestly say God has delivered more personal confirmation of my faith and His presence than I ever expected, but I had to BELIEVE first. . .

Well finally, the Bible is a progressive revelation of God. Starting out with Genesis and gaining momentum through the Old Testament. The New Testament is where it catches its "second wind" with the <u>incarnation of God</u>. The nature & mind & plan of Divinity is revealed in a wonderful way. I LOVE the majesty, character, grace, and His involvement with us imperfect humans. (Jesus was/is awesome!) One big advantage of the Bible is that it identifies the true GOD – we can say "The God of this Book" is the God I want to go with. And I <u>totally</u> understand it may not be politically correct these days to be specific & Biblical on this subject. But there are some PREMIUM benefits – see "What's In It For Me," Note 28. Then to be "blunt as a spoon" about the title question see Psalms 119:24, Proverbs 13:13 & Mark 8:38. Also 2 Peter1:4 ". . . he has granted to us his precious and very great promises, that through these you may escape from the corruption that is in the world because of passion, and become partakers of the divine nature." Choose Jesus & His Word, they are Alive. Find a Bible believing church & connect. You will find HOPE there, and PEACE.

66
THE BLESSING & THE CURSE

The above concept has fascinated me for well over 40 years. The notion that a loving God could radiate down a blessing <u>OR</u> a curse is probably an offensive doctrine to some, but it is clearly defined by Moses in Leviticus & Deuteronomy of the Old Testament. (Even the second commandment mentions it. Exodus 20:5-6 But the best B & C "nutshell" reference directly from God is Exodus 34:6-7.) Now the target audiences of those chapters were early Israelites. BUT the B & C theme is found in Old and New covenants. To define "blessing" briefly – Divine favor; to make happy; to be prosperous. The curse is the other stuff – excess problems, crisis, unhappiness, various kinds of failure. The B & C theme is actually seen about a thousand years <u>before</u> the Moses era where God says to Abraham, "Go from your kindred & father's house . . . I will bless you . . . I will bless those who bless you . . . him who curses you I will curse." (Genesis 12:1-3) The Christian church of the last 2,000 years is based <u>on Abraham's FAITH</u>, but the B & C is mentioned about 40 years earlier in Abe's life.

So why does God wish to bless people? I believe it is <u>basic</u> to His nature to <u>GIVE</u>. – (Lucky for us, God has a giving heart . . .) And there may be <u>thousands</u> of passages that suggest (and promise) positive benefits from the above dimension for Israel & believers in Christ which constitutes the "blessing" without ever using the B-word. But here are a few choice & CLEAR references to the blessing: "Blessed shall you be in the city, and blessed shall you be in the field. Blessed shall be the fruit of your body, and the fruit of your ground . . . Blessed shall be your basket and your kneading trough. Blessed shall you be when you come in and blessed shall you be when you go out." (Deuteronomy 28:3-6) And in the last few pages of the Book we have "Blessed is he who reads . . . and blessed are those who hear . . ." (Revelation 1:3) It appears that reading & cultivating the message of the Book also has a benefit.

Now the purpose of this essay is NOT to "thump the Bible," and focus on the curse. But it would be easy to do that when at page 3 of the Book we were evicted from the garden with the "curse" being mentioned by God . . . Genesis 3:17-24 And that C-word is used numerous times in the above Leviticus 26 & Deuteronomy 28 - indeed throughout the Book. Then the present moral decay & decline of our society & world with all the natural disasters, droughts, fires, murders, political dysfunction, national financial crisis, etc. etc. makes me ask questions – like, "Could a Divine curse/judgment be on the whole world?" "Is this the beginning of the end?" There is MUCH from those early chapters that indicate Divine judgment/curse from above. And plenty of information from cover to cover WHY God has displeasure with His creatures.

The problem is basically SIN which we are all born into. Man by nature turns away from God, leaving an empty place in our lives where divine presence & blessing should be. Psalms 32:1-2 KJV tells us, "Blessed is he <u>whose sin is covered</u>. Blessed is the man <u>to whom the Lord imputes no iniquity</u>." To be blessed we must deal with the sin problem. The world wants (& teaches) us to live & swim in sin so we CAN'T be blessed. This is where Jesus comes in. He came into the world to die for our sin. "Christ redeemed us from the curse . . .for it is written 'Cursed be everyone who hangs on a tree' – that in Christ Jesus the <u>blessing of Abraham</u> might come upon the Gentiles." (Galatians 3:13-14) This means that we all have <u>the option</u> of being released from the natural curse of sin. In repentance from sin & accepting Christ we can participate in the blessings God intended for his people from the beginning. Each individual can reject the spirit of this world AND its curse. Choose Jesus. He is Alive. Ask for God's Spirit & Blessing – it is a better way to go. . . see also "The Endorsement" Note 15.

67
WAXING PHILOSOPHICAL

Philosophy goes back at least 2300 years to Plato who was considered the "father" of it. An American philosopher of 1892 vintage defined P. this way – "Life involves passions, faiths, doubts, and courage. The critical inquiry into what these things mean and imply is philosophy." Josiah Royce (1855-1916) Basically Philosophy asks WHY and WHAT.

Some "Why" questions:
- Why does the toast fall off the breakfast table & hit the floor jelly side down?
- Why do little girls run & scream, while little boys torment the house pets & climb trees?
- Why do cats purr & rub your legs, while dogs bark & lick your face?
- Why is air invisible? Why is God invisible?

Some "What" questions:
- What would McDonalds be if we were all vegetarians?
- What would the U.S. be if JFK hadn't been assassinated in 1963?
- What would the U.S. be if MLK hadn't been assassinated in 1968?
- "What is man, that thou dost make so much of him, and that thou dost set thy mind upon him, dost visit him every morning, and test him every moment?" Job 7:17
- What is the purpose of re-inventing the wheel?

Now I realize the above "philosophical" questions are "small potatoes." The BIG question for me is this: Why is our country & world departing from the faith & religion of the Bible and turning to all sorts of "other" approaches to God, or no God at all. The zeitgeist of the time seems to be "anything but Christianity." Buddhism, Hinduism, Islam, New Age, & lots of others are having spurts of growth & respect while the faith of the Bible and its value system is too often suspect. Our schools & universities prefer atheism & our government philosophy seems to be shifting away from the faith of our founding fathers. We've gone too far with "separation of Church & State." The recent Supreme Court decision to endorse same-sex marriage flies in the face of the religion we came here with from Spain & England. (Tampering with the definition of marriage the way they have has probably caused <u>all</u> our founding fathers to turn over in their graves.)

The Bible was a main source of truth/right & wrong that established our western society. Our body of laws & thought parallels that material revealed to Moses in Exodus 20-23, then expanded on in Leviticus & Deuteronomy. Nowadays we seem to be getting away from our "roots" and going with atheism, false religion & "political correctness." It's not difficult to look at the track record of Israel of old and see the same patterns of decline. The Old Testament is complete w/the story. It also helps answer the big question WHY. - - "Has a nation changed its gods, even though they are no gods? But my people have changed their glory for that which does not profit." (Jeremiah 2:11) I find it interesting that people & nations with non-Biblical religions don't seem to change their false gods. But Israel & Christian people who have the Real McCoy don't always hang on to it with tenacity. We've got out of the paid-for new touring class Mercedes, and got into a rusty 1962 Volkswagon with bald tires & knocking motor that smokes. (For a word on "backsliding" see "Patterns" Note 59.) We have allowed "change," and "re-inventing the wheel." Again, WHY – and WHAT will the outcome be??

Well I don't claim or want to be a philosopher. H.L. Mencken (1880-1956) said, "There is no record in human history of a happy philosopher." – (A Mencken Chrestomathy). I just want to maximize life satisfaction, and let the "Whys" and "What's" take care of themselves. "Lord, my heart is not haughty, nor mine eyes lofty: neither do I exercise myself in great matters, (philosophy) or in things too high for me." (Psalm 131:1) Choose Jesus, He is Alive. His Salvation & Blessing answers MANY questions without "Waxing Philosophical."

Over 200 other titles: www.gospelnotes.net

68
REASONING WITH GOD

It appears to me that the human reasoning process is not always helpful – such as reasoning with a mad dog, a spooky horse, a stalling car, a teenage daughter, a drunk person, etc., etc.. All of these I have done, but is reasoning with God (or being mad at God) just another irrational thing to do?

There are some interesting cases in the Book where man did some "bare bones" reasoning with God for various reasons. Abraham's <u>audacity</u> as he faced God in Genesis 18:20-32 just knocks me out. Moses in Numbers 11:15 was so <u>frustrated</u> with the Israelites he said to God, "... kill me at once ..." Job was so bold he <u>found fault</u> with God in his lengthy discourses with his bogus comforters. Then we come to Jesus, the essence of God in human flesh, praying & sweating blood in petition in the garden before his death. (Luke 22:44) These intense examples of RWG <u>at least</u> show graphically that man can RWG & be answered by a seemingly untouchable, invisible, & IMMENSE being such as the ONLY Almighty.

Now some folks are likely to <u>lose their faith AND become mad at God</u> when Life hands them a raw deal. All folks ask God why when life gives them tragedy – lost love, lost child, death by surprise, etc. A queen of England, Anne in 1710 turned her back on the church & God because ALL of her 11 children died before adulthood. My mother had a handicap and questioned God – several times she said, "I curse the day I was born a woman." I recently came down with a form of Leukemia which has induced some RWG. (But I think if all folks could take their problems and put them in a great big common stinking pile, most would return to the pile for <u>their own</u>, rather than someone else's problems, if they had to choose.)

For "no extra charge" I should mention the <u>Five Stages of Grief</u>. People who are "Reasoning with God" are usually doing so due to a crisis situation or deep loss. Very often we go through 5 stages – 1) Denial 2) Anger 3) Bargaining 4) Depression 5) Acceptance. Sometimes the order may be different, or a stage or two missing, but the process is the same.

I believe that losing one's faith and/or becoming mad at God is not good for us, with the <u>Revealed</u> character & nature of God being what it is. He loves & cares about us . . . He is SOVEREIGN, and may allow difficult issues to come to each one of us to shape character. (See also "God's Humbling Machine" Note 201) But in this Holy Spirit age, FAITH

& PRAISE to God may be a better way to get answers than accusing God of evil intentions or ineptness. If we focus on step 5 above, we may avoid the heartburn & confusion of the previous 4. And of course we do have a spiritual enemy that can & will conspire against us. (Peter 5:8-10) Beware of him & get mad at him – NOT GOD. The mad at God syndrome just blocks answers, and the victory in Christ.

So how can a subject like this lead to a Christian appeal to faith in Christ? Well in fact, anyone who is "Reasoning with God" is on track with FAITH. I've heard preachers say that even if we are cursing God, that is a sign of hope – We're at least on the right frequency. And I do believe God has a special place in His heart for those who are "bleeding" and "RWG". ". . . He will surely be gracious to you at the sound of your cry; when he hears it, he will answer you." (Isaiah 30:19) "He giveth power to the faint; and to them that have no might He increaseth strength." (Isaiah 40:29 KJV) Choose Jesus, He is Alive. Go ahead and reason with God – it's a good thing. Answers will come according to God's perfect timing. See also "Looking Forward" Note 85.

69
THE PRAYING WOMAN

Is it true that "the hand that rocks the cradle rules the world?" Or "Nations never rise above the quality of their women." – (The Women of the Bible, Dr. H. Lockyer. Zondervan, 1967). Is it true that women pray more than men? The age old gender symbols – one with an arrow, the other with a cross might suggest this. But a quick look at even Biblical women doesn't indicate a majority that prayed. It does give several female examples of devotion & prayer – Hannah, Ruth, Anna, Dorcas, Elisabeth, Lois and of course Mary. But I can say for sure that this world knows not how much evil has been changed, and how much influence for good has been wrought by a praying mother or grandmother.

What brings proud, self sufficient, egotistical folks & especially women to pray? I believe natural devotion is rare – ADVERSITY is the element that leads to prayer. Which gender has more desperate straights than women? Having a physical disadvantage of size & strength compared to the male, then often suffering the "barefoot & pregnant" condition is surely a big factor in why many women learn to pray.

How do they pray? Well, according to the patterns of their family traditions or denomination. Protestants have their style, while the Catholic half of Christendom has its style. There may be a question as to who has the "inside track" with God. And the on-going battles between P & C in Belfast Ireland don't seem to provide the answer. (The "Belfast Boogie" only shows that prayer is being neglected.)

Here is a case of "the praying woman" type: My father's mother Oweene (long since deceased) married the original Fred about 1920. He was fond of booze & liked to beat his wife. Oweene knew adversity when she ran out of the house wounded & screaming down the street. And the great depression was in full bloom. Having 5 kids in this situation would lead any woman to pray . . . Then the abusive husband became sick & died in 1938. Then her only son, (my father) who helped support the family got drafted into WW2. He survived "bloody Omaha beach" and other battles <u>unscathed</u>, one of twelve of his 197 man unit. And I would have been twice dead if it wasn't for her prayers – dad's close calls, then mine in Viet Nam 25 years later.

Now a lot of folks thought Oweene was "too religious," talking about Jesus all the time, but I think she learned to pray & KNEW the secret that <u>God hears & answers prayer</u>. I see the fruit of her family & ALL her children have done well. And there are about a hundred grand & great grand-children. On Aug. 5, 1987 I was heading to the hospital to say "the last good-bye" when I saw an awesome cloud formation in the direction of Prescott, AZ. It was like a large group of figures (angels?) standing around something in the center ascending into the sky. I can still see it in my mind - just an extremely inspiring & unique arrangement of clouds. Thirty minutes later we reached the hospital only to have the nurse in charge tell me "she passed away 30 minutes ago – sorry." I believe God showed me <u>personally & graphically</u> just how special that "praying woman" was. And she was a Catholic.

So what's the point? The lady above wasn't perfect, but she had FAITH. And any family is very fortunate to have a mother who cares enough to pray. "We know that God does not listen to sinners, but if anyone is a worshipper of God and does his will, God listens to him" (or her). (John 9:31) "The eyes of the Lord are upon the righteous, and his ears are open to their prayer. . ." (1 Peter 3:12) I know that making a case for prayer in this hard world is tough, but it may be the only thing that can save us – on the small scale of the individual & the large scale of the nation. Choose Jesus, He is Alive – His value system and prayer is Immaculate. See Note 37 "What is Prayer?" And if you are a woman, be a praying woman – it's a better deal. . .

70

THE CHAPLAINS

These "Gospel notes" started not long after I became acquainted with "the Chaplains." I worked with them for very close to 20 years, so maybe a look at the chaplain corps is useful. Our military had chaplains from at least 1776. They are with the troops in battle & in garrison/training. Chaplains provide morale support, religious services, baptisms, weddings, funerals, counseling, suicide awareness, and just a general Godly presence in the military environment. In battle he is a comforter with the message "death is not the end." The Chaplain is quite often the most educated man around, and is a full officer type "chief", while most servicemen are enlisted "Indians" of the force. Chaps. are non-combatant & cannot carry a weapon - the assistant does that part. I was fortunate to become acquainted with them. Indeed it was a DIVINE APPOINTMENT. (see Note 151)

Chaplains have to be psychologically TOUGH due to the rejection they deal with each day. Most servicemen don't join or get drafted to be "churched" but usually the contrary. Below are some of the chaps. I worked with as an enlisted assistant.

A. This active Army character was spiritual. I SAW miracles at his hands. Several other chaps. came to his services, not to spy, but to "experience." He was a charismatic SBC.
B. This guy was a Nazarene. By accident (or divine appointment) we met & he basically gave me my first job as Chaplain Assistant. He was an inspiring & dynamic holiness preacher.
C. This chap was UMC & very liberal. While working with him I started writing "Gospel-notes" which may be part of the reason he fired me. Conservative & liberal bones don't mix too well. . .
D. This guy was a Navy officer first. Apparently NOT a man of faith, but much ego & military politics. He probably coached chap. C to get rid of me ...
E. This gentleman tolerated my zeal & confided to me that he had to go to a city dinner function and bring out our Brigade commander who was drunk & profane & on the floor. (Tough job for such a nice guy.) He also introduced me to the N.N.O K. duty. That's notifying next of kin, of their serviceman's death.
F. This senior chap. was an AME and proud to be groomed for O6

promotion. Atheist assistants were more likely to stay in his service than zealous believers like myself. He & his associate UMC chap. fire me.

G. This guy was also a senior career chap. but more of a businessman. He had 25 or so rentals in that Army town. He is the one who got me to thinking about real estate which has been a phenomenal endeavor ... Another divine appointment for sure.

H. This chap. was a reservist but totally as well educated. A fine godly gentleman, but his wife couldn't deal with the politics of the ministry, so she divorced him. After all that education & military schooling he was out BECAUSE his denomination didn't tolerate clergy divorce. Without civilian clergy endorsement the Army had to let him go too - I saw him cry.

I. Army Reserve Chap. Dale H. & assistant Bob S. were both fine characters, "a scholar & a gentleman" at least. I saw them in a dream a few days before meeting them. I had been fired in the Nat. Guard for "seemingly" false reasons, and that assistant even moved from his AR "slot" so I could have it, & continue my humble military career.

J. My last chaplain "John" was maybe the finest. A Viet Nam vet who was seriously shot then became a Portland, Oregon police officer for 15 yrs. A 300 lb belligerent female, whom he had to subdue, ruined his back. He then schooled to be a chaplain, was excellent & made it all the way to O6. Which goes to show, "you can't keep a good man down."

This incomplete list could go on & on. I will say that chaps. are generally very Godly men. Besides their chapel duties, they dealt with bizarre problems - some I couldn't mention. And the 3 times I was fired as Chaplain Assistant, I am glad BECAUSE each time God gave me a better situation in the chap. corps & at least once a permanent promotion. (God takes care of His own.)

So what is the point of this essay? Like a person has a body, mind & SOUL, the Chaplaincy is the SOUL (or conscience) of the military. Our system is well rounded & COMPLETED with the chaplaincy presence. Probably our military is the best in the world because our founders wanted the SOUL part of the system to be supported/completed. Now is YOUR soul being supported & COMPLETED? If not, why not? Jesus Christ is the "Chaplain" of this world & cared enough to die for you. Choose Jesus, he is Alive. See John 3:16 Also "The Date" Note 18, one of the earliest "Gospel-notes."

71
UGLY OR PRETTY?

"Mirror, mirror on the wall, who's the fairest of them all?" In a society & world that practically worships youth & beauty, the above title is a serious issue for most folks. And while it is true that some "ugly" folks are "pretty" inside; some "pretty" folks are "ugly" inside, the greater issue is whether life is fair... It appears that beauty gives both genders an advantage in all fields, while the normal or ugly can have an uphill battle. Business, teaching, politics, ministry, medical, legal, service – all of them, seem to favor the "pretty". Scripture says "Man looks on the outward appearance..." (Samuel 16:7)

For a professional note on the advantages of good looks on success, researchers Hamermesh & Biddle at the Univ. of Texas did a study which revealed as much as 10 percent better salary in any profession they looked at. Now if you are ugly, it's apparently a disadvantage even in court. Sociology researchers Downs & Lyons showed from fifteen hundred defendants that Texas judges impose sterner sentences on unattractive felons. (info. from "SHAM" 2005 S. Salerno) This world may show favoritism (or censure) but I am comforted knowing that God "sees" us differently. The rest of the above scripture says, "but the Lord looks on the heart." He may even show the "underdog" favoritism – see Note 26.

An age old question is whether Jesus Christ was "ugly or pretty." The best answer is Isaiah 53:2 which was written 800 years before Christ appeared before the public. "... He had no form or comeliness that we should look at him..." And John Baptist of Christ's time was described as out of style. "John wore a garment of camel's hair, and a leather girdle around his waist; and his food was locusts & wild honey." (Matthew 3:4) If God had any kind of Hollywood sense, both of those characters would have been "pretty". But God doesn't run on the theatre & political code – IMAGE is PRESTIGE is CREDIBILITY.

As regarding preaching, I once heard a Methodist clergyman say "people won't remember what you say, they won't remember what you do, but they will remember how you make them feel." Well I strike out on that score being probably in the "ugly" or at best normal category. I believe GOSPELNOTES can be a ministry tool for me – I let the Holy Spirit make the impression. Forty years ago Chaplain B of Note 70 expressed his disdain for the tract ministry. It wasn't his style to "drop them & run." Well, it's not my style either – I place them & walk away . . . And the internet connection creates a mission field practically from space.

So what is the point? Those who are "pretty" should be thankful & consider their beauty as a gift from above. For those who are lacking in "pretty" (myself included), all is not lost – God's blessing & presence can level the playing field. (And if He helps us find our NICHE we are really in position to win . . .) We should "play the hand that is dealt us," AND not fall into the "mad at God" syndrome if we happen to be less than beautiful. Then we could ask, "Does God make mistakes?" I prefer to think Father God is a gentleman, scholar, & HEALER, and doesn't make mistakes, but NOW, Mother Nature does – she even flies on a broom at times . . . I believe if we cultivate our faith & salvation in Christ, we can rise above all kinds of worldly problems including "ugly or pretty." It is true that God "sees" his redeemed people as "pretty" & blesses them whether they are fair to look upon or not. "Behold, you are beautiful, my beloved, truly lovely . . . You are all fair, my love; there is no flaw in you." (Song of Solomon 1:16 & 4:7) Choose Jesus, He is Alive. And be blessed in spite of the World's value systems. See "The World" Note 27.

72
GOD'S ECONOMICS

A preacher recently announced there were 726 sins. He is now being besieged by requests for the list by people who think they are missing something. By the looks of this day and age, it would seem that there is much value in accumulating sin. And it's true in a certain respect. You see, life is like a bank – whatever we put in our account is added to the previous balance and interest is paid on the whole figure/pile. A little bit of blasphemy here, maybe some backstabbing there, a few sex conquests, and what have you, all adds up. You say "When does the 'much value' come in?" I say it comes in right now – all negative.

Many people think the rewards of life are given at the end of the road, but that's only half the story. Every rotten thought, word, and act is recorded now and we receive interest on it now. "Be sure, your sin will find you out." "The curse of the Lord is in the house of the wicked." (Proverbs 3:33 KJV) "Misfortune pursues sinners." The apostle Paul put it this way, "do not be deceived, God is not mocked; for whatever a man sows, that he will also reap." These are hard and cold facts, but ones we should all know since they bear down on every one of us. You and I make our exciting and good plans for life and love, only to see many of them hit the rocks. Our careers sink, divorces mount, children's lives are shattered, hopes and dreams crumble all along the way. People say, "why, Why, WHY!?" My friend, God's justice (see "Divine Priorities" Note 156) is no small thing – that's why.

How much better and more practical it is to be out of debt with God and still banking with Him. He deals well on a positive basis also. "Take delight in the Lord and He will give you the desires of your heart." "He blesseth the habitation of the just." "Prosperity rewards the righteous." "Eye hath not seen, nor ear heard, neither have entered into the heart of man the things which God hath prepared for them that love Him." (1 Corinthians 2:9 KJV) Let's invest wisely in God's bank of life, and participate in "God's Economics." Right now He is saying to us, "Behold, I stand at the door and knock; if any one hears my voice and opens the door, I will come in to him and eat with him, and he with me." See also Romans 10:8-13. Scriptures referred to are Numbers 32:23, Proverbs 13:21,

Galatians 6:7, Psalms 37:4, and Revelation 3:20.

The above was written April '78 in Key West, Florida. We printed those essays on Navy paper & distributed them to the soldiers & sailors. I was the assistant for the Army Chaplain at Naval Air Station. The Army had been there since the Cuban missile crisis of '62 with four Hawk missile sites. It was very good active duty, even though my boss, "chaplain C," fired me for being too conservative. (See "The Chaplains" Note 70). My gripe then as it is now is this – if we are too focused on universalism (liberal thought) we may miss Gospel salvation, God's blessing, & maybe even heaven itself. . . Why take chances with our eternal souls? Cornelius was a devout man but lacked the apostolic message that only Jesus saves. Acts, Chapter 10. After he received the gospel & Christ, God blessed him real well . . . Andthat appears to be the New Testament pattern. Choose Jesus and His value system, they are Alive.

73

DIVINE PRESENCE

This title is truly going out on a limb for Jesus. But I don't care – I can touch subjects most preachers wouldn't touch with a long pole. So, What is Divine Presence? With a thousand faiths dealing with an invisible God, is it possible to know if we have the right "Divine Presence"? Is there a reason to care, or cultivate D.P.? Good questions for those who think.

According to the Book, God has always desired to be "present" with people. But the character Moses asked for D.P., & the concept had its most dramatic beginning. "My presence will go with you, and I will give you rest." Exodus 33:14 (Anyone who has seen the classic movie "The Ten Commandments" should admit that Charlton Heston played the "glowing" Moses quite well.) And if Moses had a glow from D.P., the transfiguration of Jesus Christ in Matthew 17 took the concept to a whole new level.

So how do those 2 characters & events have anything to do with the individual today? Well, J.C. spoke of a Counselor/Comforter/Spirit of Truth in John 14. "If a man loves me, he will keep my word, and my Father will love him, and we will come to him and make our home with him." V. 23 That is "Divine Presence." It may not have a "glow" like the above cases, but in the parameters of FAITH it is real just the same. (But I have seen that glow on people.)

"Divine Presence" is a matter of having the salvation of Christ in place in one's life. It is also the mindset of FAITH, not as much thinking on oneself & those problems, issues, limitations, etc, BUT reflecting on our Biblical God, who He is & how He has interacted with others & oneself. It is practicing this mindset. In difficult situations D.P. is KNOWING He is with me – and expecting with that divine touch, maybe I won't mess this one up . . . Some religious folks sing this song "grace, grace, grace is all I need." Well I also need a little D.P. now & then. And I want it, & I've learned how faithful our Biblical God is. D.P. IS REASSURING. I believe that things could get so rough & rude in this country/world with financial collapse & chaos at all levels that D.P. may be necessary to survive.

Cultivating "Divine Presence" – "Be still & know that I am God" Psalms 46:10 In a quiet place or at night in the sack, that sound of silence or ringing in one's ears can be thought of as the frequency of the Holy Spirit. Whether it is or isn't – prayer, praise & thanksgiving can be done & it counts the same. Walking thru the forest or any secluded place & talking to that "Counselor" cultivates D.P.. And of course – church should be a place of D.P., if not then "something is wrong with that picture."

(Psalms 16:11) "Thou dost show me the path of life; in thy <u>presence</u> there is fullness of joy, in thy right hand are pleasures for evermore." (Psalms 25:14 KJV) "The secret of the Lord is with them that fear him; and he will show them his covenant." (Zechariah 4:6b KJV) "Not by might nor by power, but by my Spirit sayeth the Lord." (John 14:6) Jesus said..."I am the way, and the truth, and the life; no one comes to the Father, but by me." (James 4:8 KJV) "draw nigh to God and He will draw nigh to you..."

If we want Biblical faith, PRESENCE, destiny, etc. we should focus on Bible teaching. Sure it is a matter of some discipline & commitment, and it is not especially fashionable. BUT – it is VALID as it ever was. Whoever learns to live in "Divine Presence" enhances their lives with something this old world knows nothing about. Choose Jesus & His Spirit – they are Alive.

74
WHY LITERAL?

The Scriptures are very interesting, and of course they are the basis of all Christian churches. The question above is asked by all who think and read those scriptures. Now there are lots of figures of speech in there because the Bible is also <u>excellent</u> literature employing simile, metaphor, and hyperbole. But is it wise to stick with only the allegorical, & mythical senses and avoid the literal sense? Many of our denominations today seem to prefer the non-literal styles of interpretation. And I believe a lot of people today lack the <u>moral</u> <u>courage</u> to associate with literal Biblical commitment & principles, fearing the social reproach or persecution factor.

So "Why <u>not</u> literal?" The problem is a handful of things; 7 day creation & young earth, MIRACLES, the devil, Christ as God, and heaven & hell. (John 5:28-29 KJV) "The hour is coming when all that are in the graves shall come forth . . . some to resurrection of life & some to resurrection of damnation." Let's face it; the MIRACULOUS is right at the CORE of most folk's objection.

Here are a few philosophers' attitudes.

- "Get rid of the miracles and the whole world will fall at the feet of J.C." Jean Jacques Rousseau (1712-1778) (what a crock.) [1]
- "A fact never went into partnership with a miracle. Truth scorns the assistance of wonders. Robert Ingersoll (1833-1899) [2]
- "In religion man denies his reason." Ludwig Feuerbach (1804-1872) [3]
- I have personally heard a liberal clergyman say, "I don't want to cut off MY head." (Incidentally, he had a master's degree in philosophy also.)

The above attitudes of unbelief <u>lead to</u> a condition in religious thought called "liberalism." John H. Newman, English Bishop 1879 produced the best definition I've seen. "<u>Liberalism</u> in religion is the doctrine that there is no positive truth in religion, but that one God is as good as another." An Orthodox Rabbi I admire put it this way. "Modern liberalism simply means becoming "liberated" from the external authority of God . . . Liberalism – rejecting God." Daniel Lapin, "America's Real War" (1999 pgs 271 & 273) Well, if we don't want to stand LITERAL it's almost certain we will fall liberal. And when the flood gate of liberalism opens, the best parts of Biblical faith are <u>at risk or</u> <u>washed away</u>. ("If the foundations be destroyed, what can the righteous do?" Psalms 11:3) Liberalism kills the very things that promote Christian VICTORY & HOPE <u>such as</u> one-way salvation, God's blessing, His personal friendship & presence, personal miracles, resurrection of the dead, streets of gold in heaven, seeing "previously gone" loved ones there, etc., etc.. All that remains is the "form of religion without the power there of" (2 Timothy 3:5 KJV), and a nothingness concept of the next life. And of course, the very common but Biblically <u>false</u> concept that, "all paths lead to the same Heaven." (See John 14:6)

So "Why Literal"? Firstly – the integrity of the Word of God is upheld. Then I would say we honor God when we give Him the benefit of the doubt. I believe FAITH & BELIEVING are God's <u>required</u> catalysts to understand Bible accounts, and see Divine action. Jesus was a <u>very special</u> character & He puts a premium on believing. At a real quick glance at just the present tense of the word "believe," there are 13 places in the Old Testament where it is used, but 108 in the New Testament. And "faith" is also a New Testament concept that is <u>dynamic</u>. God is looking for it in people. See Hebrews chapter 11. (And when we don't feel the "good stuff" but only doubts, we can say to God "help my unbelief" Mark 9:24). He helped my unbelief right at the start by showing me miracles. See Notes 7, 33, & 43. When we experience a miracle or two it will put all of the Bible in a new light, after which being LITERAL is <u>no problem</u>.

Now, do I believe literally where it says, "If your right eye causes you to sin, gouge it out...?" (Matthew 5:29 KJV) "If anyone comes to me and does not hate his own father and mother..." (Luke 14:26) "He will cover you with his feathers, and under his wings you will find refuge." (Psalms 91:4 NAS) No, <u>those</u> are figures of speech. Would I participate in venomous snake handling in church to prove the presence of the Holy Spirit? (Mark 16:18) No, I don't go there; my wife would beat me for that (LOL). All I am saying in this essay is: <u>believe the Bible</u> – <u>give it a chance</u>. (John 20:31) "these are written that you may believe that Jesus is the Christ, the Son of God, and that believing you may have life in his name." And that phrase "life in His name" is a New Testament concept that has changed people & the world for two thousand years now. Choose Jesus, He is Alive.

* Footnotes 1-3 from "The Great Thoughts" Compiled by George Seldes

75
FAITH

Faith is a girl's name – a popular one at that. While speaking of beauty, art, music & enchantment, faith LIFTS us to the realm of divinity. And being a word that has several elements and MUCH depth, it can be hard to define. An old standard Bible Dictionary (Unger's) offers this wordy def.: Intellectually, "Faith is belief or trust; especially in a higher power. Faith, viewed philosophically, must be regarded as lying at the basis of all knowledge . . . Truths or facts arrived at by logical processes . . . are held to be known because, first of all we have confidence in the laws of the human mind . . . Faith in the theological sense . . . is properly defined as the conviction of the reality of the truths and facts which God has revealed, such conviction resting solely upon the testimony of God." The following are references to faith by all kinds of characters of the past and present.

- "Faith means intense, usually confident, belief that is not based on evidence sufficient to command assent from every reasonable person." Walter Kaufmann, 1961 [1] philosopher
- "The great act of faith is when a man decides that he is not God." Oliver W. Holmes, 1907 [2] U.S. Supreme Court Justice
- "To be an atheist requires an infinitely greater measure of faith than to receive all the great truths which atheism would deny." Joseph Addison,[3] 17th century poet
- "Reason is . . . Faith on the other side, is the assent to any proposition, not thus made out by the deductions of reason, . . . as coming from God, in some extra ordinary way of communication.   This way of discovering truth to men, we call Revelation." John Locke,[4] 1690 philosopher
- "It is the heart which experiences God, and not reason. This, then, is faith: God felt by the heart, not reason." Blaise Pascal, [5] 1670 French philosopher
- "If the work of God would be comprehended by reason, it would be no longer wonderful, and faith would have no merit if reason provided proof." Gregory I, [6] 593 – Pope
- "Faith with an upper-case "F" means specifically the ability to see an invisible God as clearly as if He stood before us." "America's Real War" Rabbi Daniel Lapin (1999 pg 155)

156

From my own faith experience, and the above thinker's viewpoints, it is safe to say that faith is a very human & beautiful thing. Scripture itself speaks <u>highly</u> of faith. "Now faith is the assurance of things hoped for, the conviction of things not seen. For by it the men of old received divine approval. By faith we <u>understand</u> that the world was created by the word of God, so that what is seen was made out of things which do not appear. . . And without faith it is impossible to please him. For whoever would draw near to God must believe that he exists and that he <u>rewards</u> those who seek him." Hebrews 11:1-3, 6 (All of that chapter is FAMOUS for explaining <u>God's</u> view of faith.)

So what are some other rewards of <u>faith</u>? In a nutshell – being lifted to the "realm of divinity" (Ephesians 2:6) by the Word of God. And interesting enough, one of the names of Christ is "Word of God." Rev 19:13 His bloody salvation & Spirit truly are the beginning of Faith's reward's to the individual. But it's not a done deal there. The good stuff, or benefits of Christian <u>faith</u> are abundant. The scriptures contain hundreds of promises from God. This short essay can't list those promises, but the "blessing" is a fair summary. Then last but not least is the reward of eternal life in heaven. Faith in J.C. paves the way. "Behold I stand at the door and knock; if any one hears my voice and opens the door, I will come in to him and eat with him, and he with me." (Revelation 3:20) Choose Jesus, and His Spirit, They are Alive. Also see "What's In It For Me" Note 28.

* Footnotes 1-6 from "The Great Thoughts", Compiled by George Seldes

76
"IF I WERE THE DEVIL"

We appear to be living in perilous changing times. So many things are disconnected in the American society and the world, that folks are worried. Well, about 50 years ago there was a <u>famous voice</u> who put it all in a nutshell. Either it was just penetrating perspective or some kind of prophecy... The following thoughts were voiced by legendary ABC Radio commentator <u>Paul Harvey</u> on April 3, 1965.

"If I were the Devil... I mean, if I were the Prince of Darkness, I would of course, want to engulf the whole earth in darkness. I would have a third of its real estate and four-fifths of its population, but I would not be happy until I had seized the ripest apple on the tree, so I should set about however necessary to take over the United States. I would begin with a campaign of whispers. With the wisdom of a serpent, I would whisper to you as I whispered to Eve: "Do as you please." "Do as you please." To the young, I would whisper, "The Bible is a myth." I would convince them that man created God instead of the other way around. I would confide that what is bad is good, and what is good is "square". In the ears of the young marrieds, I would whisper that work is debasing, that cocktail parties are good for you. I would caution them not to be extreme in religion, in patriotism, in moral conduct. And the old, I would teach to pray. I would teach them to say after me: "Our Father, which art in Washington"...

"If I were the devil, I'd educate authors in how to make lurid literature exciting so that anything else would appear dull and uninteresting. I'd threaten T.V. with dirtier movies and vice versa. And then, if I were the devil, I'd get organized. I'd infiltrate unions and urge more loafing and less work, because idle hands usually work for me. I'd peddle narcotics to whom I could. I'd sell alcohol to ladies and gentlemen of distinction. And I'd tranquilize the rest with pills. If I were the devil, I would encourage schools to refine young intellects but neglect to discipline emotions... let those run wild. I would designate an atheist to front for me before the highest courts in the land and I would get preachers to say "she's right." With flattery and promises of power, I could gets courts to rule what I construe as against God and in favor of pornography, and thus, I would evict God from the courthouse, and then from the school house, and then from the houses of Congress and then, in His own churches I would substitute psychology for religion, and I would deify science because that way men would become smart enough to create

super weapons but not wise enough to control them.

"If I were Satan, I'd make the symbol of Easter an egg, and the symbol of Christmas, a bottle. If I were the devil, I would take from those who have and I would give to those who wanted, until I had killed the incentive of the ambitious. And then, my police state would force everybody back to work. Then I could separate families, putting children in uniform, women in coal mines, and objectors in slave camps. In others words, if I were Satan, I'd just keep on doing what he's doing." **Paul Harvey**, *"Good Day."*

When P. H. broadcast the above, I was barely a teenager & couldn't care less about any of it. Now some 50 years later his uncanny point of view is amazing. God help us . . .

- 2 Timothy 3:1-2 - End Times - "Understand this, that in the last days there will come times of stress. For men will be lovers of self, lovers of money, proud, arrogant, abusive, disobedient to their parents, ungrateful, unholy."
- James 4:7-8 KJV - Backsliding - "Submit yourselves therefore to God. Resist the devil & he will flee from you. Cleanse your hands, ye sinners, and purify your hearts, ye double minded."
- 1 Peter 5:8-9 - Admonitions - "Be sober, be watchful. Your adversary the devil prowls around like a roaring lion, seeking someone to devour. Resist him, firm in your faith . . ."
- Proverbs 1:32-33 - Unbelief - "the simple are killed by their turning away, and the complacence of fools destroys them; but he who listens to me will dwell secure and will be at ease, without dread of evil."

Well, as Solomon says in that first chapter of Proverbs, "he who listens to me . . .," Christ is now saying the same to all of us. Choose Jesus, He is Alive. Nothing less can save us. See also 2 Chronicles 7:14.

77

THE SHAKEDOWN

My Wife & I recently took the plane to Pennsylvania Dutch country. But, first step nowadays is the TSA lines & search. OK – shoes off, belt off, hat off, wallet & keys in the tray. Nothing in pockets, carry-on bags can have nothing resembling knives, guns, explosives, etc. Ask no dumb questions like, "do you check false teeth & underwear too?" At any rate it's understood - if you don't get thru the TSA shakedown, you don't fly . . .

Would it be possible to view life in general as a colossal shake down for sin? Is God putting all of us through a time process that illustrates the damaging effects of bad living traits such as pride, hate, blasphemy, promiscuity, devious habits, lies, greed, hypocrisy, false religion, etc.? I believe <u>Time is the agent</u> that is searching all of us. Henry Wadsworth Longfellow said this;

"Though the mills of God grind slowly, yet they grind exceedingly small.
Though with patience He stands waiting, with exactness grinds He all."

Now the scriptures have some <u>amazing</u> contrasts. One that fascinates me is the difference between some characters who have failed the divine shakedown & some who passed. Such as Korah in Numbers 16:29-33 & Judas in Acts 1:18 who failed. Then such as Enoch & Elijah who were so close to God they didn't experience physical death. Genesis 5:24 & 2 Kings 2:11. Those are <u>extreme</u> cases, of those who DON'T "fly" and those who DO "fly".

Well, we passed the TSA shakedown & made it to Lancaster county Penn. where the Amish have been living for three hundred years. The Amish (& Mennonite) came here from Switzerland-Holland to practice their religion & lifestyle. They are extreme in their determination to pass the Divine Shakedown of time. They avoid sin & worldliness "like the plague." FEW modern conveniences such as electricity, cars; and television is <u>anathema</u>. Horse & buggies everywhere with bearded male drivers. Women wearing very plain clothing & bonnets. And mostly farm living as it was hundreds of years ago. In terms of contrast – their work ethic &

austerity puts us to shame. I would say the final percentage of those "country bumpkins" who pass the Divine Shakedown of life & time is MUCH higher than the general population of America. (But I'm not planning to join them – I don't milk cows & reach way into the tail end to check the progress of the baby cow.)

So what is the point of this Gospelnote? Just this – this world truly is a Divine Shakedown, but I don't find the Christian life that difficult. God will shine a light on our sin & expect us to part with it. But even the above extreme conservatives seem to have happiness, contentment & the victory in Christ. What us "English" (outside Amish) need to do is, "Believe in the Lord Jesus, and you will be saved, you and your household." Acts 16:31 There is more of course, but that is the start of it. And it's worth it, especially considering God's blessing on Christians in this life & a better eternity . . .

- Romans 12:2 "Do not be conformed to this world, but be transformed by the renewal of your mind, that you may prove what is the will of God, what is good and acceptable and perfect."
- Colossians 3:2-3 "Set your minds on things that are above, not on things that are on earth. For you have died, and your life is hid with Christ in God."
- Revelation 3:20 "Behold, I stand at the door and knock; if any one hears my voice and opens the door, I will come in to him and eat with him, and he with me."
-

Choose Jesus, He is Alive. And "fly" with Him. See also "The Take Off" Note 22.

78
FRUSTRATIONS

One thing seems to be certain in this world, and that is frustrations. Things have a way of going haywire way too often. Murphy's Law says, "If anything can go wrong, it will do so at the most awkward time." (Was Murphy a pessimist or a realist?) At any rate, most informed folks will agree that frustrations are <u>real</u>.

- The builder – "How can there be so many government rules & regulations, then so many scheduling setbacks?"
- The Politician – "Why do folks have such good memories & remind me of all my campaign lies?"
- The brain surgeon – "We have to complete this lobotomy but the patient keeps waking up."
- The school teacher – "How can I teach this class when Johnny keeps disrupting & we can't discipline him?"
- The landlord – "You must pay the rent." Tenant – "I can't pay the rent." – (Actually nonpayment of rent is a small frustration for me – dogs have been #1.)
- The dancer – "I could dance like a ballerina if it wasn't for these corns, bunions & big feet."
- The motorist – "I just had that pricy gadget fixed and now it's going out again."
- The Italian cruise ship captain – "Just because the ship is taking on tons of water & leaning over, it can't be sinking – let's wait a little longer . . ."

Would it be a sin to ask if <u>God</u> has frustrations? If the Bible represents truth, and God has a personality, then we can be sure he suffers frustrations. Grief & sorrow are no new things for the Divine heart. I'm thinking of the fall of the human race (paradise lost) as recorded in Genesis 3. Then the flood of Genesis chap 7. Sodom & Gomorrah chap. 19, burned up for their evil habits. The struggles & battles of early Israel. The failures of later Israel. Then the rejection of their Messiah & destruction of Jerusalem by Roman armies in A.D. 70. All the suffering & pain & death of fallen humanity in just scriptural accounts is a <u>huge</u> quantity – but God has witnessed all the rest too. The sorrows of God are well spoken in Lamentations 1:12 "Is it nothing to you, all you who pass by? Look and see if there is any sorrow like my sorrow which was brought upon me, which the Lord inflicted on the day of his fierce anger." (That is also thought to be the state of God's heart when Christ was offered on the cross for our sin.)

I know it is not possible to fully comprehend God, but we can know what is revealed/ recorded. When we consider that God is love & that the world has NOT been a place of peace & love, it is clear that He has a frustrated if not a <u>wounded</u> & <u>broken</u> heart. And that sorrowing heart may shed light on why God engineered <u>the Atonement</u> (from the moment of the fall, Genesis 3:15) which brings man & God together. "God so loved the world that he gave his only Son, that whoever believes in him should not perish but have eternal life." John 3:16

To conclude I would say that frustrations are a part of life because God is also frustrated. He is frustrated with our sin & rebellious natures and wants to show us a better way. Jesus can renew each person that is willing to be transformed. It really is possible to know Christ and experience the upward path. (see Proverbs 4:18) Of course it is comforting to look forward to that place where there will be NO frustrations. For a glimpse of <u>paradise regained</u>, see Revelation 21:3-4. Someone will say, "you have to die to get there." I would answer, "you have to die anyway, why not die with HOPE?" And if you want to bring pleasure to a great big bleeding Divine heart, Choose Jesus, He is Alive. And let His salvation bring the Blessing & melt away some of your frustrations. See "The Blessing & The Curse" Note 66.

79
RUDE SURPRISES

I think us Americans are programmed from childhood to love surprises. We enjoy birthday gifts, Christmas gifts, and nice new things at Easter, etc. Then in the romance arena there is a surprise engagement ring or piece of jewelry. Then in the entertainment industry contrast & "surprise" is popular. But in this real world we also have "Rude Surprises" which usually are not lovable. Every example below is/was real.

- Incoming phone call: "You say my child did WHAT on the school grounds"?
- Your wife (husband?) put anti-freeze in the transmission by mistake. ($2500. repair bill)
- Pilot husband having heated argument with wife while flying over Florida in their private plane. She snatches keys from the ignition & tosses them out the window. $150 K airplane lost to citrus trees, but no fatalities. (just one deceased marriage)
- Incoming phone call: "You say my wife & daughter-in-law have been in an auto crash & are being flown to the hospital?"
- At the time of delivery you have twins when all the while the medical folks said it was a single baby.
- Your doctor requests a private conference, then informs you of Leukemia in your blood.
- In the middle of your auto repair your mechanic & friend has a coronary & is pronounced deceased at the hospital after failed CPR in route.

I am thankful that not all the above RUDE SURPRISES happened to me. But most of them did . . . My father who was a survivor of the great depression and WW2 as a grunt often said, "Freddy, life is not a bowl of cherries." He was right. Now he & I being acquainted with a few "rude surprises", I want to ask, "what would be the RUDEST surprise of all?"

What could be worse than going out of this life & meeting a Biblical God for personal judgment and standing there naked? Ecclesiastes 5:15 The theme of scriptures from Genesis to Revelation appears to be personal accountability to the only God, and judgment is explained & defined more clearly as the progressive revelation develops through the New Testament. The Great White throne judgment can be found close to the end. "Then I saw a great white throne and Him who sat upon it; from his presence earth and sky fled away, and no place was found for them. And I saw the dead, great and small, standing before the throne and books were opened. Also another book was opened, which is the book of life. And the dead were judged by what was written in the books, by what they had done." Revelation 20:11-12. Jesus Christ explained this also in John 12:48 maybe 50 years earlier.

Now I cannot imagine the shock of the hard-nosed atheist or normal unbeliever facing a Biblical God that he/she didn't believe existed; AND dismal prospects for eternity, not having the proper <u>robe of salvation</u> at that time. According to scripture no excuses will float. "I saw too many hypocrites in the church." "I thought my wife did a good enough job with religion in our house." "My university Profs. said we created you." "All my friends said the Bible was just myths," "My karma ran over your dogma." I know God is <u>very</u> generous & he might explain to each lost soul why they failed judgment. But I wouldn't count on that <u>because</u> of the vast quantity of available information on the subject already provided – The Bible. See a <u>penetrating</u> account of a judged soul in Luke 16:19-31 – The rich man & Lazarus.

To conclude I would admit we can expect some "rude surprises" from time to time. But the <u>rudest</u> imaginable can be avoided. It can be avoided by simply accepting the salvation of Christ. "Therefore I counsel you to buy from me gold refined by fire, that you may be rich, and have white garments to clothe you and to keep the shame of your nakedness from being seen, and salve to anoint your eyes, that you may see. As many as I love I rebuke and chasten: be zealous therefore, and repent." (the resurrected & glorified J.C. said that) Revelation 3:18-19 "Blessed are those who wash their robes, that they may have the right to the tree of life and that they may enter the city by the gate," Revelation 22:14 Choose Jesus, He is Alive. And be blessed in this life, and well "dressed" at the end of it.

80

ILLUSIONS

The world that greets our eyes & mind has interesting things. One being illusions. Some similar words are mirage, falseness, delusion, optical slip, etc. A dictionary would define illusion as "a false idea or conception – an unreal, deceptive, or misleading appearance or image. A false perception, conception, or interpretation of what one sees (or thinks)." A magician knows how to create illusions for entertainment. The following are some common illusions.

- Love & emotions are sometimes illusions.
- Fears can be illusions because most don't happen.
- False confidence on any subject is an illusion of power.
- Confidence in man – friends, associates, politicians, etc., can be an illusion because we don't really know them. We only know their facial expressions, traits, name, etc, but the REAL person is that VAST PROGRAM of memories, values, education, talents, secret desires, (demons?), etc. that are all hidden somewhere 2-3 inches behind the eyeballs.
- Paper money is a kind of illusion because it has no intrinsic value.
- "What is legal is right," is an illusion. A clergyman with 2 doctorates opened my eyes to this problem in this world. No amount of political correctness can make wrong things right, and it's another illusion to think folks can be coerced to think a certain way in a land where freedom is (or was) king.

Well are money, pride, power, status, wisdom, beauty, fame, and prestige illusions?? Maybe not, but according to the Book they may not be as important as many folks think. At a time of national decline a character named Jeremiah spoke for God, "Thus says the Lord; "Let not the wise man glory in his wisdom, let not the mighty man glory in his might, let not the rich man glory in his riches; but let him who glories glory in this, that he understands and knows me, . . ." (Jeremiah 9:23-24) A few hundred years later Christ himself said, "He who finds his life will lose it, and he who loses his life for my sake will find it." (Matthew 10:39) On the illusion of riches J.C. said "what profit is it to a man if he gain the whole world, and loses his own soul?" (Matthew 16:26 KJV)

Is FAITH itself just another illusion? Is Christ an illusion of history and the church? Is Christianity just another religion, and on equal footing with other faiths?? Actually, the others don't come close because Jesus rose from the dead, unlike Confucius, Mohammed, Buddha, all of them who rotted in their graves. And the resurrection was not a magic trick or an illusion. I know this because He touched ME Feb 20, 1972 and changed my life dramatically. I had the typical unbelief & sin in my life, but wanted answers. The Christmas story, Easter, and the A.D. calendar told me that Christ was no "illusion." I reached out to Him & have experienced that new life the apostle Paul wrote about. "If anyone is in Christ, he is a new creation; the old has passed away, behold the new has come." (2 Corinthians 5:17) I was so impressed with the spiritual awakening & "Divine Presence" that I began reading scripture with an appetite. Then for several years I memorized hundreds of texts so as to not lose or forget the experience of that other dimension that had touched me. Then in 1977 I started writing gospel notes – "The Take Off" #1, partly as another way to remind myself of "the experience." I re-read them to myself frequently.

Jesus Christ is not an illusion -- He is the answer. The Christian life is not a gimmick -- it is an adventure. The promise of blissful life beyond the grave is a gift way beyond compare. Choose Jesus, He is Alive. "Seek and you will find . . ." (Matthew 7:7)

81

THE COMMUTER FLIGHT

My wife & I recently flew in a De Havilland Turboprop from Newark, N.J. to Harrisburg, PA. I noticed that the seats were a little smaller & the isle more narrow, just overall leaner & meaner. We had 35 or so passengers and there was turbulence that afternoon. No problem there, even though I knew this same type commuter just a year or two ago went straight down & demolished a house in flames, & all passengers aboard the flight. The real problem for me was my bladder.

The small airliner was dancing around in the turbulence while I was going forward up the isle nearly falling in folks lap. Wasn't drunk but appeared to be. Reaching the lavatory up front was a relief, EXCEPT it was so small only midgets would have enough room. THEN the light didn't work so total darkness. "Deal with it Fred." I had to pee, but finding the toilet seat was a hand search that blind folks sadly are used to. Then the challenge of faith to hit the hole w/o getting the floor & my socks too . . . Finally I emerged back into the A/C isle only to have my jacket hood snag the smoke detector; anger & embarrassment? Moral of story – life can be a challenge, but w/o light everything is worse.

With the "turbulence" of this world & living w/o light, there appears to be a tendency to fall into hollow philosophy, false religion, hate & despair, bad attitude, lethargy, sinful rebellion, blasphemy & (blaming God), promiscuity, atheism, family & marriage dysfunctions, etc. Had I been more intelligent in my younger days, I might have gone to a humanistic outlook where there is no God, so self-effort can & must fix all problems. But I didn't get that far – someone was praying down God's light on me. Christ's salvation happened, then I read about that light:

- Psalm 119:105 "Thy word is a lamp to my feet and a light to my path."
- Psalm 119:130 "The unfolding of thy words gives light; it imparts understanding to the simple."
- Proverbs 4:18 "The path of the righteous is like the light of dawn, which shines brighter & brighter until full day. v.19 "The way of the wicked is like deep darkness; they do not know over what they stumble."
- John 3:19 "This is the judgment, that the light has come into the world, and men loved darkness rather than light, because their deeds were evil."

- John 8:12 "I am the light of the world; he who follows me will not walk in darkness, but will have the light of life." Jesus
- 2 Corinthians 4:4 "The god of this world (Lucifer) has blinded the minds of the unbelievers, to keep them from seeing the light of the gospel of the glory of Christ, who is the likeness of God."

Now there's a lot more on "light" from Genesis to Revelation. And if the Bible is truly the Words of God, then apparently He wants us to understand the difference between light and darkness. I found that difference over 4 decades ago, then in the commuter plane it clicked again . . . Light makes all the difference in this turbulent world. Unfortunately, too many folks avoid God's light in this world of turbulence until they "crash & burn." So sad & unnecessary.

The salvation of Christ is basically a matter of tapping into God's light so as to avoid many common problems, and eternal separation from God. That salvation is also a matter of allowing God to "shine" down on us His favor or "blessing," and a ticket into eternal bliss. (These things are explained in great detail in the four gospels by Christ Himself.) I like those free benefits – you will too. Choose Jesus, He is Alive. See also Note 28 – "What's In It For Me?"

82

CHURCH VITALITY

After 47 years of being involved in Christian churches & some of that time in full time ministry, I have made the following conclusion. While churches come in all shapes, sizes & denominations, they generally consist of three main parts: Spirituality, Social Dynamics, and Church Politics. Understanding this will help the individual find the kind of group he/she is looking for.

- **POLITICS**

  Defined as government structure, denominational loyalty, who is in power; taking sides. Church politics is in the order of that stuff we all had in first grade - "My dog is better than your dog" or "my dad can beat up your dad."
    - Example: I AM chairman of the board, deacon, pastor, etc AND YOU'RE NOT.
    - Example: Who is the most prominent family around here? We really want to know.
    - Example: No matter what miracles those holy rollers experience, we will have no part of the Holy Spirit around here . . .
    - Example: Those "OTHER" faiths are way off - they couldn't be saved. We are not like them and we do not like them.

- **SOCIAL DYNAMICS**

  Defined as getting along well with others; sociable (a social nature). Of, for, or involving friends, companionship, or sociability. Offering material aid, counseling services, group recreational activities, etc. to those who need it.
    - Example: We are right and we are all family here because we love God and each other. Of course it's better if you have a congenial personality or a prominent position in the church.
    - Example: Formal membership is expected AND adoption of our political code is mandatory. Otherwise you will not be welcome and will get the cold shoulder. The above kind of politics & social "stuff" might make for good group psychology, but it does muddy up the "water" of true religion. (See "Religion Divides" Note 32).

- **SPIRITUALITY**
  In a Christian sense, this means, being a follower of Jesus Christ & a possessor of His salvation & values, such as love, joy, peace, patience, kindness, goodness, faith, gentleness & self control. It also means having a desire to promote the values & salvation of Christ in the local community to nurture church growth. It strives toward a balanced concept of God - Father, Son & Holy Spirit. It honors the Bible as the living Word of God. It has to mean giving love & acceptance to others as God has demonstrated His love to the world. It is an act desire and a lifestyle of being close to God. It puts an emphasis on prayer, tapping into the provisions of God and living in the power of the Spirit rather than self sufficiency. Acts 1:8, Psalm 127:1

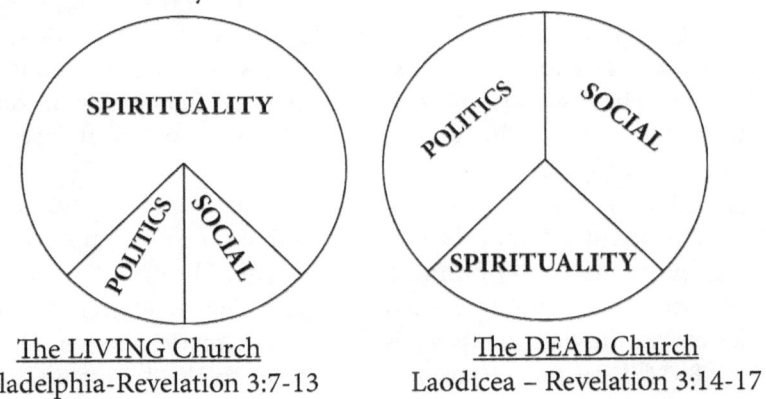

The LIVING Church
Philadelphia-Revelation 3:7-13

The DEAD Church
Laodicea – Revelation 3:14-17

Now it is true that even in a spiritual church there will be some politics and social games. The real sad story is when the church offers little more than human games. We should support churches that haven't defeated their own purpose with petty humanness. By all means be Christian and go to church. But to maximize one's growth & victory in Christ, the LIVING church is the place to be.

* Charts by F.J.S.

83

FORMULA FOR SUCCESS

What is success? Different people & cultures have other definitions of success. A place like India has a caste system which often makes our Western & U.S. definition of success impossible. No class mobility there to speak of. But here it's defined as moving up from having less to a place of having a better standard of living. Better education, job, residence, auto, & less debt, etc. And finding one's NICHE can be a real benefit in this process. Consider the five elements below as a concise & simple Formula For Success.

- <u>Self Discipline</u>. Just the word Discipline is key here. All military services promote this because they know without discipline, their force will be disorganized & weak at all levels. Personal focus on one's time schedule, exercise, and diet is vital to one's personal success. See Proverbs 12:1, 2 Peter 1:5-9
- <u>Knowledge.</u> Any advanced society promotes education. So does any success oriented family. Is it surprising that Solomon (supposed to be the wisest man ever) promoted knowledge? "Does not wisdom call, does not understanding raise her voice? . . . For wisdom is better than jewels, and all that you may desire cannot compare with her." Proverbs 8:1 & 11 Then moving on in that chapter to V. 22-36 is a CLASSIC treatise on the value of wisdom. And a couple hundred years later, one Hosea had this tidbit for us. "My people are destroyed for lack of knowledge . . ." 4:6
- <u>Work</u>. The human body is made to work. Whether we are sweating it out over books, or doing physical labor, it just feels good to work & accomplish something useful each day. Not many folks get far without work. Sadly our U.S. society is not emphasizing the work ethic these days. Nowadays work is almost something to be ashamed of. I believe it is <u>honorable</u> & God blesses it. Even the man who cleans gutters & the motel maid has God's attention.
- <u>Money Management</u>. They say there are two ways to have more money. Make more, or spend less. Whether that's true or not, I have found that we either manage our money or it manages us. And there is a credit system that promotes debt. Scripture says "the borrower is the slave of the lender." Proverbs 22:7 Slavery never ended – it just changed its suit. Now it's a voluntary predicament thru excessive debt. I believe

minimizing our rent, mortgages, auto debt, credit card debt, etc. is vital to success & freedom. For a simple & effective way to reduce credit cards, take 2 at a time & scrape dog poop off the floor with them. Throw them in trash with the poop.

- Faith. Last but not least, we have a world famous Book that says MUCH about faith & personal success. And our adversary can promote all kinds of falseness about God's material blessings if people just remain ignorant of Bible teaching. See Psalms 37:25-26, Proverbs 13:21, 16:20, 28:19, Matthew 6:33, Philippians 4:19 Then FAITH can be the catalyst to help the individual find their NICHE – that position where he/she can be MOST successful. See "Faith" Note 75.

When the above elements are blended together in a person's life, they will promote the maximum success for that person. And I find it interesting that SUCCESS & FREEDOM are married together. I like the feeling of Freedom, so if I could give one more tidbit to this "formula for success" I'd say minimize housing cost to be within one's means. That major budget item is what appears to keep millions of folks in the "hand to mouth" mode till they die. See "Home Ownership Technique." Note 106.

Now for no extra charge, a recent thinker said this, "Judge your success by the degree that you're enjoying peace, health, and love." H. Jackson Brown, Jr. ("Life's Little Instruction Book", 1991 #304) And in order for this Formula For Success to be a true "Gospel-note," it has to connect with ultimate success. That is being received into God's best place when we "meet the undertaker" – (inevitable for all.) It's sad when folks have real success & die, but without Christ's salvation. "What profit is it to a man if he gain the whole world, and lose his own soul?" J. C. - Matthew 16:26 KJV   The best WIN-WIN is to have success in life, THEN go to heaven. Jesus said, "I am the way, and the truth, and the life; no one comes to the Father, but by me." John 14:6 Choose Jesus, He is Alive.

84

UNHOLY CATS

Unholy cats wrangle at night & come between you & peaceful sleep. When we were in Oklahoma the "unholy cats" would raise hell right outside our bedroom window. Once I ran out the side door grabbing a boot which worked well to quiet the fuss. In the morning when fetching my flying boot, there were patches of fur pieces where the cats had been tearing each other apart. <u>On another level of thought</u>, there appears to be "unholy cats" that come between us and peace with God. Below are some insights on the problem of SIN.

- Five great enemies to peace inhabit within us: viz., avarice, ambition, envy, anger, and pride. If those enemies (unholy cats) were to be banished, we should infallibly enjoy perpetual peace. Francesco Petrarca 1350, Italian poet. "The Great Thoughts" 1925 George Seldes
- The seven sins are: wealth without works, pleasure without conscience, knowledge without character, commerce without morality, science without humanity, worship without sacrifice, and politics without principal. Mahatma Gandhi
- "Sin is first pleasing, then it grows easy, then delightful, then frequent, then habitual, then confirmed; then the man is impenitent, then he is obstinate, then he is resolved never to repent, and then he is ruined." Robert Leighton <u>christian-quotes.ochristian.com</u>

According to the Book, sin (unholy cats) do keep us from peace with God:
- "Are the consolations of God small with thee: Is there any secret thing with thee?" Job 15:11 KJV
- "If I regard iniquity in my heart, the Lord will not hear me;" Psalm 66:18 KJV
- "He who conceals his transgressions will not prosper, but he who confesses and forsakes them will obtain mercy." Proverbs 28:13
- "Those who regard worthless idols, forsake their own mercy." Jonah 2:8 KJV (Jonah is an amazing piece of Scripture – besides the big fish story which blocks many folks from reading it, it has concepts of <u>faith</u> beyond many other Old Testament books.)

Now this Gospel-note has considered un-holy cats. So logically it would imply that there are <u>holy</u> cats too. But I know of none, EXCEPT Jesus Christ, who is actually a LION – "the Lion of the tribe of Judah, the Root of David, has conquered . . ." Revelation 5:5 A lot of thinkers question whether J. C. really did conquer at all. After all, He was executed with criminals . . . BUT when we consider that Christ was/is mentioned as a person hundreds & thousands of years <u>before He was born</u>, then at his birth announced by <u>angels</u>. ". . . and you shall call his name Jesus, for he will save his people from their sins." Matthew 1:21. Then of course the miracles & brave death & resurrection of Christ. Then how Christ has become the story of history from A.D. 1, it is clear we are dealing with a "lion." See Note 7 "I Saw The King." From the moment of my glimpse of Christ, I was impressed with His majesty & bearing like a "lion."

Well as I reflect on the "unholy cats" of this world, and how they can keep us from peace with God, <u>it is just too sad</u>. So many young people want to associate with the aggressor, but miss the fact that Christ is a "lion" – just usually a friendly & patient one. And there is a symbolic "clip" of the believer in Christ in Isaiah 11:7, where the tamed lion is symbolical of the natural man subdued by grace & salvation. (Unger) Let's not allow our sin (unholy cats) to ruin our peace with God, and His blessing. "Behold, I stand at the door and knock, if anyone hears my voice and opens the door, I will come in to him & eat with him, and he with me." Revelation 3:20 Choose Jesus, He is Alive.

Over 200 Titles: www.gospelnotes.net

85

LOOKING FORWARD

Having just returned home from a tragic funeral for a beautiful 20 year old girl who apparently took her own life, I touch this subject with a serious & heavy heart. "Looking forward" can be a matter of survival, especially in tough times. Other words for L.F. are hope, desire, trust, confidence, reassurance, optimism, advance, headway, improvement, growth, etc, etc. One Orison Marden said this "There is no medicine like hope, no incentive so great, and no tonic so powerful as expectation of something tomorrow." (wiseoldsayings.com) Then a thinker named Nestell Bovee added this, "When all else is lost, the future still remains." (brainyquote.com)

Besides the sad & terrible loss of the young girl above, I have personally tended to dwell on negative issues too often. And we all have failures, disappointments, & bad memories of all sorts in our past. I know that dwelling on that "stuff" is a downer which can lead to years of heartache. We need to "look forward," not backwards. Lying awake at night "reminiscing" usually doesn't solve ANY problems, only kills sleep. And there are psychotic powers of the mind which like such hopeless "fodder" to focus on which can lead to depression, despondency, despair & even SUICIDE. (See "Dragons of the Mind" Note 185.) The preacher today 13 Feb. '14 said, "The hole we dig may cave in on us." And if there is a spiritual adversary, he would want all people to fall into bad thinking habits & FOCUS on past "negatives." (after all, his purpose is to "steal, kill, & destroy" John 10:10 KJV)

God offers a simple method of "looking forward." "Whatever is true, honorable, just, pure, whatever is lovely, gracious, if there is any excellence, anything worthy of praise, think about these things." Philippians 4:8 If we must look back, it's more useful to recall the good memories, AND the power of God in our lives – answered prayer, personal miracles He has given, etc. "Count your many blessings . . ." And I realize we may not have the power to make the resolution to think on things positive – a "new lease" of thought. But Christ's salvation & Holy Spirit really does empower the individual to that "new lease." And absorbing scripture is excellent because many Biblical stories & principles are VERY positive in

nature & outcome. Jesus Christ finished that John 10:10 KJV reference above this way - ..."I am come that they (you) may have life & have it more abundantly."
- Psalm 37:4 "Take delight in the Lord, and he will give you the desires of your heart."
- Jeremiah 29:11-12 "I know the plans I have for you, says the Lord, plans for welfare and not for evil, to give you a future and a hope. Then you will call upon me and come and pray to me, and I will hear you."
- Romans 8:28 "We know that all things work together for good to them that love God, to them who are the called according to his purpose."
- Romans 15:13 KJV "Now the God of hope fill you with all joy and peace in believing, that ye may abound in hope, through the power of the Holy Ghost."

To conclude let me say first to myself, "look forward," it will make today better. It will also ditch a lot of worrying, which can never fix the past. God wants us to cultivate joy & peace & the victory. "Looking Forward" is a better mindset by far. Choose Jesus and His Salvation, they are Alive. See also "Mindset of Victory" link 103.

On the subject of Depression, despondency, & Suicide, I recommend "A journey Through PTSD", by Dr. John J. South. His book is recently published by Life Guides Press, Mesa, AZ. ISBN: 978-0-9965066-0-1 Dr. South has a few decades experience as a police officer & Army Chaplain counseling in Suicide Intervention, Crisis, Grief, and the combat induced PTSD. I served with him as chaplain assistant from '93-95 in the US Army Reserve, & give him & his book four stars for excellence.

86

DEATH BED CONFESSIONS

Is a Death Bed Confession a matter of a jailbird admitting to crimes just before he dies? No – generally it's a matter of hiding behind an excuse system for decades, but planning to commit to God's salvation at the end of life's journey. I believe a host of folks think this way. And Human nature has a problem with death in general – Sigmund Freud (1856–1939) said, "No one believes in his own death, or, to put the same thing in another way, that in the unconscious every man of us is convinced of his own immortality." (Interpretation of Dreams, 1915) So we put it off. "Manyana is good enough for me." But eventually the serious "date" arrives. Is putting off Christ's salvation to the end a good idea?

I remember an individual who was old and classically in the "delay mode." He was my mother's father (now deceased) – 71 years older than myself. When I was about 12 or so I recall asking him why he didn't seem to have any religion being so close to the pearly gates? <u>His excuse was</u> "Cain killed Able, then went to the land of Nod & took a wife, the Bible is just myths." (Genesis 4, but easy to answer – they lived long lives and were kissing cousins.) Gramps just got older & even though he was a decent man & worked for a living, he might not have known the error of the Death Bed Confession. God is looking for a decision without DELAY or filibuster.

- John 10:27 "My sheep hear my voice, and I know them, and they follow me; and I give them eternal life . . ." Jesus C.
- 2 Corinthians 6:2 "Behold, <u>now</u> is the acceptable time; behold, <u>now</u> is the day of salvation."
- Hebrews 2:3 "how shall we escape if we neglect such a great salvation? . . ."
- Hebrews 3:15 ". . . <u>Today</u> if you will hear my voice, harden not your hearts, as in the provocation."

Daniel Webster said this "The bed of death brings every human being to his pure individuality, to the intense contemplation of that deepest and most solemn of all relations - the relation between the creature and his Creator." Well, my friend & grandfather kept putting it off. He got older & dementia set in. Some of it was real sad. . . Some preachers believe that putting off God to the end is a foolish plan & indeed scripture says this clearly. (take a look at Proverbs 1:24-32) <u>But on the other hand</u>, the blood & grace of Jesus has <u>infinite</u> power to save – even the senile. I wasn't able to see my grandfather his last few days on this planet, but my missionary friend Dick Lytle <u>went for me</u> & Gramps was open to Christ's salvation – he prayed the sinner's prayer. One of my favorite memories is a Spiritual dream (Joel 2:28) that came several years after he died – maybe 20. I saw my deceased mother in heaven playing an organ when from behind a corner my grandfather showed his (younger) face & smiled at me. God is good . . .

Now on the subject of Death Bed Confessions I would say to anyone who is planning one – BE CAREFUL, the risk is great. I am positive there are millions now in hell who danced around the question of eternal salvation till it was too late. And even if they just squeeze in, they miss becoming acquainted with an awesome God <u>in this life</u>, and His Blessing. The better plan is to accept Christ's salvation "today" without playing games with God. Choose Jesus, He is Alive. "Behold, I stand at the door and knock; if any one hears my voice and opens the door, I will come in to him and eat with him, and he with me." Revelation 3:20. See also Note #17 "Concerning Quicksand".

FIVE C'S OF ROMANCE *

We recently were on a tour bus in Shanghai, China with a tour guide who was apparently a victim of romance. She volunteered the info that Chinese women are looking for a man with five C's. Cash, Credit, Condo, Car & Career were the important things for a good relationship. Now I would suspect there are other important things in Chinese marriage, but she placed an emphasis on those five.

In the relationship between Christ and His bride (the church or believer), there are also 5 C's of "Romance", Christ the bridegroom, and the church or believer being His bride. (God's analogy, not mine - Isaiah 54:5, Ephesians 5:23) The five C's are Caring, Contrition, Commitment, Continue, and Conduct.

- Caring – People desiring to "hook-up" with God need to care that Christ was God in the flesh. Jesus said, "Have I been with you so long, and yet you do not know me, Philip? He who has seen me has seen the Father; how can you say, 'Show us the Father'?" John 14:9 They should care that the killing of Jesus was for their sin & salvation. They should care that God left us the record of the event, and that it is accurate & reliable.
- Contrition – People approaching God should have a humble heart towards Him. "This is the man to whom I will look, he that is humble and contrite in spirit, and trembles at my word." Isaiah 66:2b
- Commitment – A relationship, to God & Christ as in a marriage, is not much good without commitment to the cause. Commitment also means convene or congregate – attend church & support it.
- Continue – To get the most "for our money" we need to be in the "ball game" for the long haul. Too often we attempt to accomplish things by "fits & starts."
- Conduct – Someone once said that "personal conduct is supremely important," anon. Christians need to have high standards of conduct because we are watched carefully by the world. See Note #36 "What is Hypocrisy?"

To the above five C's of spiritual romance could easily be added <u>Consignment</u> which means to entrust or deliver. Christians have a <u>great</u>

privilege to turn over their problems to a Christ who is big enough to take them (and alter them) for our good. (Philippians 4:6)

All the above C – words combine to define godly character and a long-term relationship with Christ. Could it be that Christ is wounded & frustrated w/"romance" as was the Chinese tour guide? (Imagine what He has gone thru then & now dealing with us un-lovely humans.) Could it also be that He will bless His people with good "stuff" if they make an attempt to please him with good character traits? "Take delight in the Lord, and He will give you the desires of your heart." Psalms 37:4 "Behold, I stand at the door and knock; if any one hears my voice and opens the door, I will come in to him and eat with him, and he with me." Revelation 3:20 "Romance" with Christ is not only a divine reality, but it's also a "trip." A trip to a good place at that. Choose Jesus, He is Alive.

* Romance quote of the day "At the touch of love, everyone becomes poetic."

88

DOG EAT DOG *

I've been told that this world of ours is a "Dog Eat Dog" world. I grew up in South Phoenix, Arizona where things were no different. My mother related an incident to me that occurred in the back yard next door. Those folks had 3 dogs which were not fed especially well & were hungry – real hungry. A smaller dog strayed by & squeezed in the fence gate to make friends. The resident pit bulls killed the smaller dog, then pulled it apart – "tug of war" style. At which time the 3rd resident hungry dog grabbed parts that fell out of the middle & ate them. It was sad that Mom had to witness that canine altercation by those neighborhood "pets" especially since she was such a polite & delicate lady who loved dogs.

Well our world is also prone to "dog eat dog" in human arenas. How about the family; where sibling rivalry can be "dog eat dog?" How about the work place? How about national politics, where Democrats & Republicans are constantly hostile to each other? It's almost like us Americans have two separate governments with very different agendas, that hate each other. And between religions there is plenty of tension. Someone once said "in a town that has 10 religions there will be harmony, but if only 2 they will fight – "dog eat dog." Even between the different factions of Christianity there is tension & bickering. The apostle Paul said "If you bite and devour one another take heed that you are not consumed by one another" (Galatians 5:15). That was a clear warning against religious "dog eat dog."

I find it interesting but sad that the Jewish Messiah, who was predicted in scripture to come to the nation of Israel, but when He did, there was a serious "dog eat dog" political & religious climate waiting for Him. Jesus was very careful to fulfill all predictions and do teaching, lots of healings, feeding THOUSANDS with a few loaves & fish, walking on water/calming storms, RAISING DEAD at least four times, etc, etc. In spite of it all, the religious leaders (Pharisees & Sadducees) arrested Jesus; then took Him to the Roman leaders who occupied the promised land at that time. To add "insult to injury" at Christ's trial they incited the crowds to ask for a known criminal to be released & crucify Jesus.

Now I have always been one to ask "why" too often. And when I ask why is this such a "dog eat dog" world? I get some comfort knowing that God in the flesh Himself (John 14:9) came here to experience the "ugliness," knowing there would be an altercation. But I get more comfort knowing that in Christ's death & resurrection, God's salvation & Spirit are released to the believer. That salvation package has numerous benefits that help to lift the individual above the fray. (See "What's in it for Me?" Note 28) Daily walking with Jesus can also help avoid the "pit bulls" of this world. (See "Divine Presence" Note 73) Then of course Faith is the key or catalyst that activates the whole process. (See "Faith" Note 75)

The ultimate solution to dealing with a "Dog Eat Dog" world such as ours is to die & go to heaven. (But most folks prefer to postpone that solution as long as possible – me too.) But Christ did discuss & explain heaven/eternal life in detail: "He who believes in the Son has eternal life" (John 3:36). "In my Father's house are many rooms; if it were not so, would I have told you that I go to prepare a place for you?" (John 14:2). The gospel of John contains lots more on the Eternal Life subject.

Finally I should say in this "Dog Eat Dog" world we are not likely to change it much, considering the nature of man & what is in the air (Ephesians 6.) But we can be changed ourselves by the touch of Christ. And that makes a huge difference. Choose Jesus, He is Alive.

* This title & illustration is a "guy thing," and could be offensive to sensitive minded souls.

89

CONCERNING RESALE

Resale is a concept usually found in business. After the customer buys a product or service, additional related items are presented. Many industries have resale. Well, we like cruise ships, & you can get real trip ticket deals, but then on board run into all kinds of "resale" stuff. Shops galore, jewelry on tables, professional portraits, expensive body massage, specialty restaurants, art auctions, port tours, ship tours, detox systems, casino, roving bar sales and more ways to sell more to the customer. Sometimes too much resale can be bothersome, but generally it just "comes with the territory." And all cruise lines have "resale," and the ship keeps moving along to the destination. Those determined to maximize their trip have faith in the Captain & the destination. They don't allow "other" agendas to spoil their trip.

Does the "resale" picture have a parallel in the spiritual/religious arena? The individual hears the simple gospel message – God loves us, sent His Son to die for our sin, man/woman repents & accepts the gift & is saved. He/she then finds a church group to be part of the "family of God." Then the "resale" kicks in. "Now you need church 3 times a week." "If you don't tithe you are robbing God." "Good Mormons get married in the temple." "It's right to eat fish on Fridays." "We Adventists really should be vegan." "To be really filled with the Holy Spirit you should speak in tongues." etc. etc. Some groups just have too much "resale." I think the spirituality of Christianity tends to break down in the midst of the well meaning "people-ness" & politics found in most denominations.

Now being a "customer of God" and participating in the salvation of Christ is a very good thing. (Lots of folks have been so convinced that they have died for their faith.) And most of thinking Christendom will admit that some of their group's doctrines & emphases can be excessive & bothersome. But the ship/denomination keeps moving toward the destination even with some excess baggage.

Is there a way to deal with the "resale" without abandoning ship? It's a sad fact that many who make a decision to follow Christ give up the "good fight" & fall away from the Lord. Some quit for reasons similar to those above. I believe seekers of God should expect & accept some issues (& people-ness) along the path. Frustration, inconvenience, challenges, etc may just come with the territory. (I think the Christian life is supposed to be a bit tough.) But <u>a focus on the Captain (J.C.) & the Destination</u> can be the winning mindset. Don't let religious "resale" spoil your "cruise."

- "He hath shewed thee, O man, what is good; and what doth the Lord require of thee, but to do justly and to love mercy, and to walk humbly with thy God? Micah 6:8 KJV
- "For by grace are ye saved through faith; and that not of yourselves: it is the gift of God: Not of works, lest any man should boast. Ephesians 2:8-9 KJV
- "Therefore let no one pass judgment on you in questions of food and drink or with regard to a festival or a new moon or a Sabbath. Colossians 2:16
- "Not by works of righteousness which we have done, but according to his mercy he saved us, by the washing of regeneration, and renewing of the Holy Ghost; which he shed on us abundantly through Jesus Christ our Savior;" Titus 3:5-6

Choose Jesus, He is Alive. "Cruise" with Him and be blessed on the way to the Destination. See also Note 59 "Patterns."

Over 200 other Titles: www.gospelnotes.net

90
GIFTS & RIFTS

This is a reflection on human character. Now everyone likes gifts, and it seems that God has bestowed/endowed most all folks with something extra in some area of talent. Athletic talent, musical/singing voice, personal charm, math wizardry, mechanical, etc. But scripture does explain the natural gift phenomena. "He has given gifts to men . . ." (Ephesians 4:8). A lot of church denominations put an emphasis on spiritual gifts. Now is there another side to this "coin?"

I believe there is a balance in nature at all levels & I ask, Do people have foul gifts also? Something like inborn rifts of character from an early age? "Even a child is known by his actions" (Proverbs 20:11). We were in a McDonald's restaurant yesterday in Hawaii, April '14 where a young lady was blowing her RAGE & profanity LOUDLY in the manager's face because of some fault with her sandwich. As she left passing close in front of me I noticed a black eye – probably from an earlier scrape with someone else. We sat down to drink our coffee only to notice a young man at the next table who obviously thought he was a female. (The Aloha & Mahalo islands have people problems too.) Now Christian theology teaches that people need to be lifted/redeemed from the natural "unsaved" human condition (Acts 4:12.), which is fine & good. But I suspect that even after God's cleansing touch of salvation we still have residing in our character some raunchy natural "rifts of slime." But I don't blame God for their origin – they are the product of a fallen world.

There is a place in the Book that sheds light on this. "I suspect there may be quarreling, jealousy, anger, selfishness, slander, gossip, conceit, and disorder" (2 Corinthians 12:20). Other references mention much worse "rifts." And could there be an un-holy spirit that hangs around people & cultivates their natural bad traits or fallen instincts? (If it's not so, then we have to rewrite the New Testament because it's full of encounters with evil spirits. Read any couple of pages & you will see info on demon activity & their products – character rifts & chaos. Especially in the four gospels where Jesus Christ is interacting with people.) Even so, we are still responsible for our actions. "The devil made me do it" could be true, but he is not prosecuted yet. And as for the on-going debate whether born again Christians can be possessed by demons; I think not, but they can be oppressed by them, and residual bad traits can sometimes flare up.

People who care & desire to live above the sins of humanness can be discouraged. (Myself included.) So what can we do? First, admit that negative traits are natural. "If we say we have no sin, we deceive ourselves and the truth is not in us." 1 John 1:8 Second, realize that the purpose of life in general is a character test (Acts 17:26) which is a serious proposition from God himself – it's supposed to be tough down here. Third, maybe God wants us to be <u>humbled</u> by our stubborn character roots (& demons?) so we can be more usable by Him in the long run. "If we confess our sins, he is faithful and just, and will forgive our sins and cleanse us from all unrighteousness" (1 John 1:9). Fourth, don't give up. Quitters lose by default. In some races just crossing the finish line "warm & breathing" is a success. "Fight the good fight of the faith." "Submit yourselves therefore to God. Resist the devil & he will flee from you. Draw near to God and he will draw near to you. . ." (James 4:7-8)

Finally I'd say, true repentance & acceptance of Christ's salvation generally gives folks power to <u>enhance</u> their good gifts & <u>suppress</u> their bad ones. See also "Roots" Note 31. "But to all who received him, who believed in his name, he gave power to become children of God;" (John 1:12). Choose Jesus. He is Alive. See also "Dragons of The Mind" Note 185.

91

THE BROTHERHOOD

I've always been impressed by the brotherhood of police. And cops seem to know their own kind – even by instinct. Recently on a cruise ship we met an 83 year old retired Jewish cop named Joe. He said he was just approached by another old retired cop who said he could see an <u>aura</u> & just knew he had been a police officer. Well, Joe "Tarzan" had been in the Orange County, CA police dept. for 35 years. Maybe Firemen & some elite servicemen (not me) are also included in the Brotherhood. Members of these institutions have a <u>common bond</u> & <u>work together</u> to achieve goals such as <u>survival training</u>, <u>commitment to integrity</u>, <u>peacekeeping</u>, <u>exposing/con-trolling the troublesome</u>, etc.

- A little Police Brotherhood slogans/trivia -

- Power, strength, resolve; together we make the thin blue line stronger.
- Us versus them – good guys/bad guys – protect & serve
- The blue line is what police stand on & protect.
- We are the barrier between anarchy and a civilized society, between order & chaos, between respect for decency, and lawlessness.
- On a lighter note – Joe "Tarzan" would go out on his front porch & call his kids home for dinner with a Tarzan call – and his was the best I've ever heard. (And I got it on my camcorder.)
- On a serious note – a cop cousin of mine here in Arizona had to go into a dwelling where a female police officer had killed her 2 small children & then herself with her service revolver. He said that was the toughest thing to deal with.

Is there another brotherhood like that above? I have considered and studied the spiritual brotherhood of believers in Christ for over 40 years to conclude that it is truly real. Fellowship is a more fitting word as "There is neither Jew nor Greek, . . .there is neither male nor female; for you are all one in Christ Jesus." Galatians 3:28 The aura may not always be visible but is truly present due to being "born again" in the salvation (body) of Christ. (John 3:3) And Christians can often recognize their own kind by instinct. There are many denominations in this fellowship/brotherhood, but there are genuine Christians in all groups. These "called out" folks have a common bond in Christ & work-together to achieve goals such as training in righteousness/godly living, how to survive & maintain the fruit of the Spirit – "love, joy, peace, patience, kindness, . . ." Galatians 5:22. They also expose evil & the works of the enemy (Ephesians 5:11) They are determined & committed to the cause of Christ which is to stand w/Jesus & influence the world for truth & integrity. They look forward to a nice (eternal) retirement where the chaos, dysfunction, & evil contortions of this world cannot enter. (Revelation 21:3-4) The old gospel song "Onward Christian Soldiers" (words by Sabine Baring-Gould, 1865) contains a clear statement of purpose. Lyrics omitted for brevity.

Well, not all of us can be in the brotherhood of police, but we can ALL be in the fellowship or family of God. It is not that difficult to turn from the pursuit of ego & worldly values to Reconciliation & the values of God. And if J. C. was God in the flesh, we can see him as the Chief of Police or Captain of the force. ". . . If anyone hears my voice & opens the door, I will come in to him and eat with him, and he with me."(Revelation 3:20) See also Joshua 5:14 & Hebrews 2:10. For a glimpse of the Chief see Note 7 "I saw the King" Choose Jesus, He is Alive.

92
BALANCE OF NATURE

This is a concept I've noticed for a lot of years. It seems that there should be a balance between hot & cold, light & dark, fast & slow, smart & dumb, luck & unlucky, wet & dry, good & bad, etc. When one extreme is evident & dominant the other shows up to produce the "balance of nature." My uncle who was a Judge & Coroner in Arizona said his County would run smoothly for a good while; then bang, deaths in series of three. Other examples below:

- A long season of normal seasons & weather, then a tornado or hurricane or drought.
- A long season of good stable economy, then a recession or depression.
- How about the 777 airliner loaded with people that crashed in San Francisco in July '13; nearly all survived. Then the 777 that crashed (?) south of Malaysia in March '14; all perished.
- The motorist with a good driving record for decades, then falls asleep at the wheel or gets T- boned.
- The gambler with good luck for a long spell, then lose it all in one evening's gaming.
- Liberace & other extremely talented musicians, but gay or psychotic in personal life.

The concept B. of N. I have noticed in many aspects of life. But as a Bible student, I see it in the Book too. In the garden we had perfection, but the serpent/tempter appeared. Job went from boom, to bust, back to boom. The Israelites went from captivity in Egypt to freedom in the Sinai desert. The centuries of the Judges saw <u>contrasts</u> & extreme swings in Israelite integrity & then faithlessness. The centuries of the Kings saw the same cycles. Then of course when the Messiah appeared, we see the people generally for Christ, but at His trial they changed & asked for a murderer. Another "balance of nature" will be the <u>contrast</u> between the first advent of Christ (AD 1 or so) & the second (any time now.) "Behold, my servant shall prosper, he shall be exalted and lifted up, and shall be very high. As many were astonished at him – his appearance was so marred, beyond human semblance, and his form beyond that of the sons of men – so shall he startle many nations; kings shall shut their mouths because of him; for that which has not been told them they shall see, . . .they shall understand."

(Isaiah 52:13-15)

    This essay is not about the second coming of Christ, but it will be the most intense contrast/balance of nature ever. The point of this short message is that the contrasts we see all around us – physical, political, spiritual, financial, inter-personal, etc. are what life is made of. But things even out – storms pass over. And if you feel that this <u>big harsh confusing world</u> wants to smash you like a bug, be encouraged that God is ultimately in control & uses extremes & contrasts to shape character. He wants to lift you & me to new heights in spite of the contrasts.

    When we have faith & look to Christ for answers, a healthy <u>balance</u> can appear. In the salvation of Christ & His blessing & hope of eternal life, there is a kind of peace & "balance" this world can't understand. "Peace I leave with you; my peace I give to you; not as the world gives do I give to you. Let not your hearts be troubled, neither let them be afraid." (John 14:27) And for those souls stressed & discouraged by negative trends, think about Oral Robert's (1918-2009) main slogan – "Something good is going to happen to you." God is a good God with a good plan for those who believe. "I know the plans I have for you, says the Lord, plans for welfare and not for evil, to give you a future and a hope. Then you will call upon me and come and pray to me, and I will hear you." (Jeremiah 29:11-12) Things will even out in your life and mine. See also Romans 8:28 Choose Jesus, He is Alive.

93
IN DEFENSE OF P. D.

Is P.D. a matter of public drunkenness? No. Is P.D. political deception? No, I'm not impressed with Machiavellian politics & don't want to defend it. This short essay IS about the controversial thought in Christianity of the <u>Prosperity Doctrine</u>. That is the notion that part of God's blessing of the redeemed is prosperity – get close to God & He will help you do well. And it's a hotly debated subject. Some opponents of the prosperity doctrine are so opposed to it they are like Hitler <u>in that</u> he would occasionally fall on the floor in a rage & chew on the carpet, practically foaming at the mouth. (LOL) Possibly, part of the reason folks have strong objections to it is due to some money raising techniques televangelists have used. Maybe their extravagant lifestyles also rub folks the wrong way. Sure, the prosperity doctrine could have a bad reputation . . .

Now I am a fairly simple minded guy, but I don't want to base my thinking on what someone else is saying or doing. And my early doctrinal position didn't really include much on the subject of money. But I did start giving to the Christian cause right after meeting the Lord in about '72. And I was poor & tight so every dollar was a sacrifice . . . I did notice that money or time given to the "cause" seemed to return to me. (Luke 6:38) And that <u>spiritual law</u> hasn't changed in the 45 plus years I have practiced it.

So, logically the issue of the Prosperity Doctrine leads to the question: should sincere Christians who are redeemed, born again, saved, confirmed, baptized, sanctified, polarized, or whatever – should they enjoy the fruit of their labor, or practice austerity? I think of Mother Theresa who would be given a nice carpet for her upstairs apartment for a touch of class & comfort. She would throw it out the window to the street below. Or how about the Amish, who believe autos & electrical appliances are too "worldly" to be righteous. (While I respect the austerity of those above, I believe a lot less folks would commit to Christ & His Church if they thought it meant sleeping on a bed of nails.) I think in this free country we should have a few comforts – especially if we have earned them & paid our taxes – to God & Caesar . . .

It may be in order to mention C. I. Scofield's definition of salvation: "The Hebrew and Greek words for salvation imply the ideas of deliverance, safety, preservation, healing, and soundness . . ." He does not directly mention prosperity. My gospel note, "What's In It For Me" link 28, is in effect MY definition of Christ's salvation. Neither do I mention prosperity. But we both suggest it in essence.

In the Bible there are VERY prosperous cases. Like Job, Abraham, David, Solomon, Matthew, probably Luke, and many others. Of course they are NOT my examples – Jesus is. And His advice on the subject seems to be – practice restraint with reason – be neither too poor or too rich – money should be a tool, not a god. Here are some Bible passages on the subject:

- Proverbs 13:21 "Misfortune pursues sinners, but prosperity rewards the righteous."
- Proverbs 16:20 "He who gives heed to the word will prosper, and happy is he who trusts in the Lord."
- Matthew 6:33 "But seek first his kingdom and his righteousness, and all these things (food, clothing, etc.) shall be yours as well."
- 2 Corinthians 9:11a "You will be enriched in every way for great generosity, . . .
- 3 John V.2 "Beloved, I pray that all may go well with you and that you may be in health . . ."

Finally I would say the Prosperity Doctrine is a subtle part of God's blessing, but I would never put an emphasis on it. However, I do have reason to believe God is faithful to His Word. His salvation package and blessing are amazing, and they are worth looking into. Choose Jesus and his Value System, they are Alive. See also 2 Chronicles 16:9, Psalms 37:25-26, Proverbs 10:22, Habakkuk 3:19, John 10:10b, Philippians 4:19.

94

TWO PICTURES

I wonder if some parts of life could be reduced down to "two pictures". For example, in U. S. politics – maybe a picture of George Washington & Abe Lincoln. Then in theater – a picture of Judy Garland & John Wayne. Then in your family – maybe a couple favorite pictures of your kids at a cute age. I have a favorite picture of my two sons age 5 & 8 where they are COVERED in mud - one happy & the other sad. The second favorite is of my daughter age 6 (with family) at the Grand Canyon edge 3 feet behind them.

Would it be possible to reduce the Bible down to just "two pictures." Two concise passages that show God's nature & policy & plan for humans? In the Old Testament I would choose that sobering passage spoken direct to Moses at the time of the 10 Commandments. "The Lord, The Lord, a God merciful and gracious, slow to anger, and abounding in steadfast love and faithfulness, keeping steadfast love for thousands, forgiving iniquity and transgression and sin, but who will by no means clear the guilty, visiting the iniquity of the fathers upon the children and the children's children, to the third and the fourth generation." (Exodus 34:6-7) That has content & depth beyond any other – in fact it may be the summary of the whole Old Testament. That would be picture #1 for me. Then in the New Testament we have Jesus giving a lengthy discourse which concludes with, "God so loved the world that he gave his only Son, that whoever believes in him should not perish but have eternal life. For God sent the Son into the world, not to condemn the world, but that the world might be saved through him. He who believes in him is not condemned; he who does not believe is condemned already, because he has not believed in the name of the only Son of God." (John 3:16-18) Picture #2 for sure.

Now it is sad that people today too often have a "picture" of God & His plan that disconnects humans from Divine accountability. And the common false picture of God makes Him our invention, just all loving with many roads to heaven – any path will do, or no path at all. We are all O.K. as we are. But the Exodus & John "pictures" above reveal a very different and Biblical concept of the living God. He is merciful, & gracious, to those who love him . . . but holds sinners responsible for their sin AND remembers all of it, visiting consequences of rebellion even to people's posterity. (Yikes – that's not in today's liberal religious agendas. See Note 66 "The Blessing and the Curse.") The LOVE of God is shown in the GIFT to this world of Christ as the Lamb of God & the solution for sin & its consequences. An old divine, Louis T. Talbot D.D. said this: "His love & mercy are made manifest not in that He overlooks sin – but in that He died, the just for the unjust – on Calvary." (God's Plan of the Ages 1936)

As I reflect back on my favorite pictures of my cute children, it occurs to me that those boys all covered with mud, is actually the way God sees all humanity (Romans 3:23). And my cute daughter 3 feet from the edge of the Grand Canyon is typical of all natural souls – "tottering on the brink" one heart beat from eternity (see Luke 16:26 & context ". . . between us and you a great chasm has been fixed: . . .") For anyone interested in God's "picture" of salvation, please consider these thoughts from the Apostle Peter:

- Peter 1:23 "You have been born anew, not of perishable seed but of imperishable, through the living and abiding word of God;"
- Peter 3:21 "Baptism . . . now saves you, not as a removal of dirt from the body <u>but as an appeal to God for a clear conscience</u>, through the resurrection of Jesus Christ," This reference may be a bit controversial, but that can be a good thing.
- 2 Peter 1:4 ". . . he has granted to us his precious and very great promises, that through these you may escape from the corruption that is in the world because of passion, and become partakers of the divine nature."

And for a "picture" of the future <u>glory</u> of the Christian's destiny see Revelation 21:1-4. Another old divine offered this: O Ye who would enter the glorious rest; and sing with the ransomed the song of the blest; the life everlasting if ye would obtain; ye must be born again." (W.T. Sleeper 1819-1904 Regeneration) Choose Jesus. He is Alive. And be blessed <u>in time & eternity.</u>

REALISTIC EXPECTATIONS

"Realistic Expectations" applies to anything: In music, will I ever be a famous singer or concert pianist? In athletics, will I/you ever be on a Wheaties box? In academics, not many get their doctorate . . . Now this short essay is about being a realist. And as a realist, should we expect greatness & action in our lives & Christian faith, or mediocrity? A lot of folks believe that unreal expectations in any endeavor leads to disappointment & feelings of inadequacy.

Taking a brief look at scripture reveals a totally different spiritual world & human interaction with it. Old Testament prophets & MAJOR miracles, then Jesus Christ in the New Testament & the Apostles and more major miracles leading to Christ's resurrection. But what about TODAY? What is reality in the Christian faith or value system?

I believe there is a range of Divine Manifestation to us – maybe 0 – 10. Some folks expect 0 from life & God, so they get 0. But given the NATURE of God & faith, we should go for the jackpot of "10". Expect "10", accept "5", and don't lose faith or hope if "0" seems like the answer. I think God is the boss – His answer is either yes, no, or wait. And if we get the "0" too often we might need to ask if Christ's salvation is actually in place, - or- is there a sin blocker? "We know that God does not listen to sinners, but if anyone is a worshiper of God and does his will, God listens to him." John 9:31 (See also Note 121 "Bad Luck Pills")

From my 47 years experience with Christ's salvation, "Realistic Expectations" is expecting God to act. He just does. Perfection (or "10" all the time), no. Faith & believing, yes. And faith, believing, trusting, WAITING on God is the stuff that honors God. He is looking for it in us. In that "faith climate", it is realistic to EXPECT things from God. Luke 18:7-8 "will not God vindicate his elect, who cry to him day & night? . . . I tell you, he will vindicate them speedily." My faith experiment from the start nearly always promoted more manifestation than I really bargained for. Mark 11:23 – 24 puts expectation in a nutshell; "Truly, I say to you, whoever says to this mountain, 'Be taken up and cast into the sea,' and does not doubt in his heart, but believes that what he says will come to pass, it will be done for him." Therefore I tell you, whatever you ask in prayer, believe that you receive it, and you will." Jesus said that for us to ponder, & I'm sure "mountain" is a figure of speech for major obstacle or problem.

Now I have seen believers in Christ fail the Faith & get mad at God when He doesn't live up to their expectations. See "Reasoning With God" Note 68. Some situations are tougher than nails & sometimes prayer doesn't seem to soften or change things. But we should let God be sovereign, & assign the fault with us not Him. The truth is: <u>I don't have to understand</u> all the whys. The missionary who got me started on the Christian Way said "If you don't understand a certain (doctrine or experience), don't worry just go on." And I have learned that life is made of mountain tops & Valleys – we won't always be in a valley. (Psalm 23 suggests this.) And then when riding a bicycle, the road is usually not all uphill.

My conclusion is this: <u>As a realist</u>, I have found God to be faithful to His word. Therefore as Paul says, "Be careful for nothing; but in everything by prayer and supplication with thanksgiving let your requests be made known unto God." "I can do all things through Christ which strengtheneth me." Philippians 4:6 & 13 KJV We can still apply these spiritual laws and EXPECT Divine answers. I don't limit God – I'm His kid, and He likes me. See "My Miracles" Note 33. Choose Jesus, He is Alive.

Many other titles: www.gospelnotes.net

96

WHAT'S IN THE BLOOD?

This is a question that has several meanings. From a medical standpoint it's vital to know that all the good elements are in balance, and that the evil elements are being controlled. From a legal standpoint it may be important to know the quantity of such elements as alcohol, cannabis, cocaine, etc, etc. From a nationalistic standpoint someone might say, "those traits are due to Irish blood" (or Cuban, Russian, Asian, etc.)

Possibly the most interesting (and famous) man ever on this planet was Jesus Christ. So just what was in His blood? The main element in His blood from a theological point of view is ACCESS TO GOD. And theologians have wrestled with Atonement as the key teaching of the Book. It is defined as the covering over of sin, the reconciliation between God and man. "Repugnant though it may be . . . the fact remains that the Bible is a blood drenched Book. From the hour God made coats of animal skins for fallen Adam & Eve, down to the millennial day, blood is seen as the purchase price of access to God." Herbert Lockyer. [1] In the garden we see animal blood; shed to provide those skins to cover Adam & Eve after the fall. Animal blood sacrifices were done at the time of Moses to show the Atonement for early Israelites. They looked forward in time to the perfect Lamb of God – Jesus Christ, because "it is impossible that the blood of bulls and goats should take away sins." Hebrews 10:4

Now, if it is so important that we all access/connect with God by the blood of that one Man Jesus, how can it have the power to do this for all mankind? Simple – that blood of Christ was the blood of Deity – or VERY royal blood. ". . .Thou wast slain and hast redeemed us to God by thy blood. . ." Revelation 5:9 KJV "But now in Christ Jesus you who once were far off have been brought near in the blood of Christ." Ephesians 2:13 (Of course, this essay only begins to touch the subject of Atonement.)

Well, I had a glimpse of that atoning blood. On the evening of my renewal in Christ experience (20 Feb '72), I retired for the evening feeling the spiritual "high". Then a "downer" memory came up. Several years earlier another 13 year old kid & myself had vandalized a small Baptist church. This memory just surfaced, & I felt terrible about it. I called the missionary even though it was real late, & expressed my feelings to him. He said, "just, go back to bed & 'plead the blood of Jesus' over this memory." I didn't kneel – just laid in the bed & prayed quietly. Out of nowhere, that crimson blood came down in small & large droplets for a long while – probably till I fell asleep. It was some kind of vision I think, but a beautiful & mysterious experience. The next AM I had no worries about the bad memory, but I did notice my cigarette habit was GONE, and my conscience was sensitive like never before. That experience was 47 years ago. If anyone wants to know why I write these Gospel-notes, that "blood" event is probably much of the reason.

So, "Access to God, the most sublime of privileges, has been purchased at a great price, the blood of Christ." Myer Pearlman.[2] Have YOU reached out in faith to claim your share of that Access? "Behold, I stand at the door and Knock; if any one hears my voice and opens the door, I will come in to him and eat with him, and he with me." Revelation 3:20 Choose Jesus, He is Alive. And His blood is still working to save. See also Note 7 "I Saw The King".

1. "All the Doctrines of the Bible" 1978, Zondervan Publishing House; pg. 188
2. "Knowing the Doctrines of the Bible" 1981, Gospel Publishing House

97
WAS JESUS GOD ?

Dr. Macartney, an author said, "The two characters of history about whom more books have been written . . . are Napoleon and Jesus Christ. ("What Jesus Really Taught", Clarence E. Macartney, 1879-1957) But what a contrast . . . Napoleon shed rivers of blood upon which to float his ambitions. The only blood Jesus shed was his own, which He poured out upon the cross, for the redemption of mankind." <u>Napoleon himself</u> says, "I know men, and I tell you, Jesus is not a man . . . the death of Christ is the death of a God. I tell you, Jesus Christ is God."

Now <u>theophanies</u> are striking Old Testament appearances of J. C. <u>thousands</u> of years <u>before</u> Mary gave Him a mortal body. "Biblical scholars identify, 'The angel of the Lord', 'The angel of his presence', 'The angel of the Covenant', as Christ, the Son of God, in pre-incarnate manifestation." (Dr. H. Lockyer, All the Doctrines of the Bible, pg 38) There are <u>at least</u> nine cases of theophany starting in Genesis thru Zechariah. Then the 105 names of Christ shed light on His greatness. See Note #46. Our calendar is divided between BC & AD. Then consider the world-wide impact of the Christmas & Easter holidays. Then according to scripture, Jesus was <u>born of a virgin.</u> This doctrine is one of the most vital to Christianity, and to the Godhood of J. C. It was predicted by the prophet Isaiah 600 years B.C. (7:14), and announced by the angel Gabriel to Mary herself. Luke 1:26-35

Theologians see a <u>profound</u> union between J. C. and the scriptures. And the "Word of God" is also a name of Christ. John 1:1 & 14 "In the beginning was the Word, and the Word was with God, and the Word was God." "The Word became flesh and dwelt among us, full of grace and truth." The scriptures are extremely important because THEY give the knowledge of Christ. People who bash the Bible are undermining their own prospect of peace and relationship with the real God. We see in those scriptures that Jesus the Christ assumed Divine Prerogatives: <u>Omnipresence</u> – Matthew 18:20; <u>Power to forgive sins</u> – Mark 2:5-10; <u>Power to raise the dead</u> – John 6:39, 11:25; Proclaimed Himself <u>Judge of man's eternal destiny</u> – John 5:22. Just looking at those EXTREME claims of J. C. gives us a choice with <u>no middle ground</u> – either He was a lunatic, or He was & is God.

If Jesus was God and He was rejected & executed by people, could that be a major factor why this is such a hard & evil world? And if it seems like Christ/God is generally aloof from people & this world it may be because Christ got such a brutal rejection & condemnation from man's religious & political systems. We "duked" Him – <u>not wise</u>. Being God & the author of all creation, then murdered by man! The irony is too much for anyone who thinks.

Now I know "people believe what they want to believe", but for me (& millions of others), believing Jesus is God is based on the above logic, AND personal revelation. We have lots of reasons to believe to the point of KNOWING. Sadly, most of the world's population <u>simply don't know</u> – maybe they don't even care. But IF most of that population did KNOW the transcendent & inimitable Christ, this planet would not be nearly the mess it is. Please let me offer a few refs. that seem to be right on target:

- Matthew 28:18 "All authority in heaven and on earth has been given to me." – The risen J.C. said that.
- John 12:44-45 "He who believes in me, believes not in me but in him who sent me. And he who sees me sees him who sent me."
- John 14:9 Jesus said to him, "Have I been with you so long, and yet you do not know me, Philip? He who has seen me has seen the Father; how can you say, 'Show us the Father'?"

This short essay is not to deny the Trinity – Father, Son & Holy Spirit. It just says that Jesus was truly God in the flesh. But when He died, God didn't die – Christianity was launched or inaugurated. And the world has been changed since then. Have YOU been changed by Jesus? If not, why not? Psalms 34:8 "O Taste and see that the Lord is Good: <u>blessed</u> is the man that trusteth in him!" KJV Choose Jesus, He is Alive. See also Note #7 "I saw the King"

98

GRAVITY

What is gravity? We know we have weight & are subject to the pull of the earth. Is gravity a kind of magnetism? Is it a product of <u>huge mass & heat</u>? Scientists say the core of the earth is nickel & iron which gives earth its magnetic field. It is 1800 miles beneath the surface - about 4400 miles in diameter & it's very hot. Now our moon is 2160 miles in diameter, so the earth core is about twice the size of the moon . . . And gravity pulls everything – rocks, wood, water, metal, even air. Now at 35,000 feet in an airliner (this was written in a Boeing 767) you will still have gravity. You walk the isles, sit in a seat, eat & drink, use the lavatory, wash face & hands in the sink, etc. The whole concept of gravity is a mystery if you think about it.

Now applying "gravity" to the much greater dimension also fits. If God exists at the core of the universe, He should have a "pull" on his creation – esp. humans. Having <u>enormous mass & warmth</u> (love), we may have no choice but to gravitate towards Him sooner, or later. People are hopelessly religious by nature. There are about 19 major world religions which are subdivided into a total of 270 large religious groups, and hundreds more smaller groups. Christian Scripture says "no one can come to me unless the Father who sent me <u>draws</u> him; . . . John 6:44. That is the <u>true</u> "gravity" of God. (And yes, there are some false religious "pulls" out there – a lot of them . . .)

I remember from the age of about 6 some kind of "pull" towards truth & integrity which I resisted with a passion till 18 or so. (The world has a way of neutralizing the gravity of God.) But then I heard the gospel of Christ & began to think about Scripture concepts. I was <u>drawn</u> to the realism in the gospels. The character of J.C. & his dealings with the people of Palestine revealed they were <u>just like us</u> in this day & age. As those folks of 2000 years ago reached out to Jesus, so did I – I gave Him a chance. (But He was reaching out to me BEFORE I reached out to Him – "gravity" & mystery.)

Well, as Newton learned that the apple falls direct to the ground because of gravity, those <u>drawn</u> by God will learn that Divine Gravity <u>pulls</u> folks to an experience with a living God. And I believe anyone who has read this far is being pulled to Christ even now. Even <u>you</u>. And please don't waste too much time reading "Gospel-notes" – go to <u>the meat of the matter</u>

& read the Gospels of Matthew, Luke & John. The Acts & then get into the Epistles of Paul – Romans, Corinthians, Galatians, etc. The Psalms are also intense reading from the days of David. To learn of those scriptures is to touch & feel the SOURCE of Divine gravity. And I learned a long time ago that He is amazing to deal with. The faith dimension is something people should not neglect or resist. (Doing so is something like shooting oneself in the foot.) See "Faith" Note 75.

- "My sheep hear my voice, and I know them, and they follow me; and I give them eternal life, and they shall never perish, and no one shall snatch them out of my hand." John 10: 27-28
- "Behold, I stand at the door <u>and knock</u>; if anyone hears my voice and opens the door, I will come in to him and eat with him, and he with me." Revelation 3:20
- "For those whom he foreknew, he also predestined to be conformed to the image of his Son . . . And those whom he predestined he also <u>called</u>; and those whom he <u>called</u> he also justified; and those whom he justified he also glorified. Romans 8:29-30 (A favorite ref. of our Calvinist friends, but it does speak of Divine "gravity".)
- "If you confess with your lips that Jesus is Lord and believe in your heart that God raised him from the dead, you will be saved." Romans 10:9
- "To thee they cried, and were saved; in thee they trusted, <u>and were not disappointed</u>". Psalms 22:5

Finally, as Newton discovered that the apple lets go & falls to the ground, so we can "let go & fall to God." Let go of carnal pride, ego, lame atheist arguments, worldly values, slothfulness, etc. & gravitate to Christ's salvation & power & blessing & eternal bliss. Choose Jesus, He is Alive.

99

TOO MANY QUESTIONS

Not enough answers. But this month, September 2014 Time Magazine asked many rare questions and even attempts to answer them. Such as: When will we go to Mars? How much hair is on your head? What is the most addictive drug? Are we there yet? Are you smarter than a teenager? How many guns are in America? What's the world's perfect sandwich? How many private jets do Americans own? How many prisoners believe in God? When is the Bible most given as a gift? When does the princess save the world? What is the meaning of life? Why are we here?

Now I found Time's answers to be interesting at least. A couple questions of my own are these: How old is God? Where did He come from? And I know we can't answer those, but Time's "<u>What is the meaning of life?</u>," can be addressed from a Biblical viewpoint. Acts 17:26-27 comes by Divine inspiration & reveals "He made from one every nation of men to live on all the face of the earth . . . <u>that they should seek God</u>, in the hope that they might feel after him and find him." That is possibly the most concise answer to life the world's books offer – and I know lots of folks won't touch it BECAUSE it's a Bible reference. (But all intelligent & logical minds should at least give the Bible and God a chance to answer questions.)

If we can accept that scripture above, then the next question is this, How do I make peace, and connect with God? Jesus Christ being God in the flesh was uniquely qualified to show humanity the answer to that question. One of the MANY things He said was "I am the way, and the truth, and the life; no one comes to the Father, but by me." John 14:6 Then He died as the Atonement for our sins. Accepting these Bible truths is very basic to our connection. I would suggest <u>to any new seeker</u> to open the New Testament to the gospel of John chapter 1, and lay your hand on that page & say "Lord Jesus, I want your salvation & Holy Spirit, please draw me into it" see also Romans 10:9. Then get into a Bible believing church if you want to grow as a Christian.

The individual's purpose/meaning of life has to be <u>enhanced</u> by the spiritual connection above. And scripture does bear this out for those who read it. "I know the plans I have for you, says the Lord, plans for welfare & not for evil, to give you a future and a hope. Then you will come to me and pray to me, and I will hear you." Jeremiah 29:11-13 Too many Christians are bashful about God's touch & don't expect much personal involvement in their lives. My experience has been "very real", & I am convinced God radiates down on believers a lot of good stuff (See Note #28 "What's In It For Me".) While much of the purpose of life is a Divine character test to see what we are made of, I believe God at the same time leads people into their best <u>niche</u>. And that is the "place" where we maximize happiness & joy, while minimizing heartburn & strife. "But the path of the righteous is like the light of dawn, which shines brighter and brighter until full day." Proverbs 4:18

    Now we all have a less than perfect body, mind, & local situation, but a healthy attitude is priceless - "A cheerful heart is a good medicine, but a downcast spirit dries up the bones." Proverbs 17:22 And of course all can be "saved" and live in God's favor/blessing. We may always have more questions than answers, but we can have <u>some</u> of the best answers, & be victorious with God's help. "The secret things belong to the Lord our God, but what is revealed belongs to us and to our children forever. . ." Deuteronomy 29:29 Choose Jesus, He is Alive.

100

COMMON CONUNDRUMS

I think I've learned a new word. Conundrum means riddle or <u>unanswerable question</u>. And naturally the more we think, the more "Cons." we find. Recently I was presented with three questions that are troublesome for some:

1. The New Testament says that Jesus is the only way to salvation. Therefore, did ordinary people before Christ have no means of salvation/heaven? (And there is the question of remote souls <u>after</u> Christ that couldn't hear the Gospel/Resurrection message.)
2. Jews are the chosen people of the Bible, but B.C. were they left out because Jesus hadn't yet visited the earth?
3. Both Old Testament & New indicate that being good (righteous) is most important. So if we are real righteous already, why do we need belief in J. C.?

Those three questions are common obstacles to faith, so I want to attempt an answer. But using logic AND scripture will be necessary so it's important to accept scripture as authoritative. I believe <u>there has to be</u> an authoritative "basis of truth" in this world, or ANYTHING goes in religion, and we continue in ambiguity. See 2 Timothy 3:16-17. If the Bible is not the words & work of God, then we just "spin our wheels" trying hopelessly to answer tough questions, or conundrums.

1A. God is just being SOVEREIGN in his choice of the revealed Messiah/Jesus only pattern we clearly see in scripture from cover to cover. (He could have chosen anything . . . imagine God requiring us to do handstands & smoke stogies as the prerequisite – LOL) And man is/was accountable to his SOVEREIGN Creator for the light he had at any point in world history. Those gentiles that lived thousands of years B. C. did have more oral tradition & less true scripture, but they had a conscience on line with God. It's how they lived with their light & conscience, and obeyed the laws of good & evil that gave them approval or censure from God. Ref. Romans 2:14-15 (please look it up). Then faith & love are major factors of divine approval. Romans 3:29-30, 13:10.

2A. Jews are clearly God's chosen people. But B.C. they looked forward to the Jewish Messiah. From the garden we have the first hint of that

Messiah in Genesis 3:15, and it's that "savior" all B.C. devout Jews looked forward to in time to be approved. Another key is revealed a couple K years later – it was the FAITH of Abraham that justified those early Jews, see Romans 4:3. Also there is a penetrating reference in 1 Peter 3:18-20 about the pre-resurrection Christ (those 3 days He was dead) going to the nether world & preaching to B. C. souls waiting to accept or reject the gospel. (heavy stuff) So those in question 2 above who appeared to be "left out", were preached the gospel to. Also Ephesians 4:9 suggests this.

3A. From the beginning, scripture reveals the honorable nature of God – truth, justice, love, giving, etc. Of course He expects us humans to choose those virtues (righteousness). But Christ is the highest revelation of God & He had a lot to say on other subjects too. Possibly the most important was the central position of His Atonement. See John 3:14-15 for starters. Then we have an account in the book of Acts where Peter was told by God to go to "Cornelius . . . a devout man who feared God with all his household, gave alms . . ., and prayed constantly to God." 10:1-2 Cornelius was righteous as they come, but he needed the gospel message of Jesus & His Atonement to be "complete" in God's eyes. Clearly, true righteousness was not enough, even for him.

Now in addition to being confounded and conundrumized (I invented that word), by the issues above some folks are troubled by churches pushing constant forgiveness for sins. And that could be a good thing because we are fallen creatures. (Remember the boot we got in the garden.) Scripture teaches us to confess our sins & get forgiven (ref. 1 John 1:9). Lucky for us God is about forgiveness. Confess sins & get forgiven – then repeat the cycle. At least Christians acknowledge the sin problem. And of course there is a fine line between a little sin/slips now & then, and rank hypocrisy. See Note #36 "What is Hypocrisy?"

Well to finish this essay, don't let pesky questions block faith in Christ too long. We only have so many days to make our peace with God. No one knows when their last day will be . . . Choose Jesus, He is Alive. Cultivate his amazing salvation & blessing, and laugh at "Common Conundrums". See also "Quicksand" Note #17 – written 40 years ago by yours truly.

Many other Titles: www.gospelnotes.net

www.ingramcontent.com/pod-product-compliance
Lightning Source LLC
Chambersburg PA
CBHW021405290426
44108CB00010B/392